AN EMBARRASSMENT OF RICHES

*Tapping Into the World's
Greatest Legacy of Wealth*

ALEXANDER GREEN

WILEY

Published by John Wiley & Sons, Inc., Hoboken, New Jersey.

Published simultaneously in Canada.

For general information on our other products and services or for technical support, please contact our Customer Care Department within the United States at (800) 762-2974, outside the United States at (317) 572-3993 or fax (317) 572-4002.

Wiley publishes in a variety of print and electronic formats and by print-on-demand. Some material included with standard print versions of this book may not be included in e-books or in print-on-demand. If this book refers to media such as a CD or DVD that is not included in the version you purchased, you may download this material at http://booksupport.wiley.com. For more information about Wiley products, visit www.wiley.com.

Library of Congress Cataloging-in-Publication Data:

Green, Alexander, 1958-
    An embarrassment of riches : tapping into the world's greatest legacy of wealth / Alexander Green.
        pages cm
    Includes bibliographical references and index.
    ISBN 978-1-118-60882-1 (hardback); 978-1-118-64656-4 (ePDF);
    978-1-118-64655-7 (ePub)
        1. Money—Moral and ethical aspects.   2. Wealth—Moral and ethical aspects.
3. Conduct of life.   I. Title.
    HG220.3.G737 2014
    178—dc23
                                                                        2013024665

Printed in the United States of America
10 9 8 7 6 5 4 3 2 1

This book is dedicated to the memory of Anna Compton Taylor

The good life is a process, not a state of being. It is a direction, not a destination.

—Carl Rogers

CONTENTS

PART THREE: A WEALTH OF UNDERSTANDING

PREFACE

You may not know it, but you are one of the richest human beings ever to walk the face of the earth. Though you have done nothing to earn or particularly deserve it, you are the inheritor of an incredible legacy of wealth, a genuine embarrassment of riches.

This may seem a bit presumptuous. After all, I probably don't know you personally. And even if I do, I haven't taken a peek at your bank accounts, brokerage statements, or 401(k). I haven't seen your home, what you drive, or how much you own. And your income, assets, and liabilities are really none of my business. Yet I still know you to be exceedingly rich. If you're skeptical, I understand. Like a lottery winner whose ticket is lost in some upstairs drawer, you can't claim your fortune—or appreciate it—if you aren't aware of it.

I will make my argument in the Introduction and offer supporting proof in the more than fifty essays that follow. Along the way, you'll discover that your life is richer, fuller, more beautiful, and far more fortunate than you previously imagined. If I do my job, you won't only feel wealthier but profoundly grateful.

So let me make my case . . .

INTRODUCTION

Everyone thinks about money. Few think about it more than I do.

That's not because I'm selfish, greedy, and materialistic. (Okay, *maybe a little*.) At various times over the past three decades, I've worked as a research analyst, stockbroker, investment adviser, portfolio manager, and financial writer.

Today, I am the Chief Investment Strategist of the Oxford Club, a private investment club dedicated to helping investors achieve and maintain financial independence. And we've had some success. The independent *Hulbert Financial Digest* has ranked the investment letter I direct—*The Oxford Communique*—among the best-performing newsletters in the nation for more than a decade now.

Wealth, of course, is a subject that interests almost everyone. Money makes things happen; it gives us choices. Since few want to live circumscribed lives, the pursuit of wealth is universal. Money allows us to achieve our dreams, whether you define that as education, opportunity, independence, luxury, security, or peace of mind. It's freedom, power, and opportunity rolled into one. As a result, there is a huge market for financial advice—and I'm fortunate to have a few hundred thousand readers who tune in regularly. Almost every day I can be found—either online or in print—weighing in on stocks, bonds, funds, interest rates, currencies, or commodities.

What is the real advantage of all your saving and investing? As I see it, there are three primary benefits:

1. If you have money, you don't have to worry about it. This isn't guaranteed, of course. I've known plenty of high-net-worth individuals who agonized over their finances and worried about losing the nest egg they'd taken a lifetime to build. Still, if you have money and manage it conservatively, your worries should be few. Fretting about your investment returns is a lot less stressful than wondering how you're going to make this month's rent.

2. Money gives you freedom to pursue your passions. You can spend your days engaged in activities that you find absorbing and satisfying, that you feel you're good at—or make you feel like you're doing good. This doesn't just happen in retirement, incidentally. A measure of financial freedom gives you the ability to swap into a new job that may be less lucrative but more fulfilling.

3. Money buys you time with family and friends. Your most valuable resource is your time, not your bank statement. And nothing contributes to personal happiness more than seeing family and friends regularly. Money gives you the wherewithal to go out to dinner with buddies, take a vacation with the kids, or go to the concert with your significant other. In my view, money is put to the best use when it is spent making memories, not loading up on more stuff.

However, financial security remains elusive for many Americans. The 2013 Retirement Confidence Survey (RCS), the longest-running survey of its kind, revealed that the percentage of workers who feel confident they have enough for a comfortable retirement is near record lows. Most Americans have too little in retirement savings and remain pessimistic about the future. In a recent poll by Yahoo! Finance, 41 percent said, "The American Dream is lost." Only 45 percent believe their kids will be better off than they are. Other surveys show that a significant percentage of us believe life is tough, the future is dim, and the country is decidedly on the wrong track.

This is understandable in some ways. Our society faces serious problems, including war, disease, corruption, poverty, nuclear proliferation, terrorism, and political dysfunction in Washington. No wonder Americans are in a foul mood, especially if this dour perspective—one cycled 24/7 by the national media—is an accurate representation of the state of the nation.

But it isn't. The media delivers the world through a highly distorted lens, emphasizing tragedies, accidents, and problems. A recent study showed that more than 90 percent of the articles in the *Washington Post* had a negative slant. Television is even gloomier—and far more sensational.

It's not hard to understand why. News media companies exist to generate profits. To do that, they need advertisers. To attract advertisers, they need viewers. And to grab viewers, they scare the pants off them, setting their amygdalas alight with news of terrorist attacks, sensational crimes, natural disasters, and other unsettling developments.

And we don't just *hear* about accidents and natural disasters; we see immediate live footage that is recycled continually throughout the day. From a media standpoint, bad news is good news. If a factory closes, that's a story. If a factory opens, it's not. Of course, no one wants to hear about the planes that didn't crash and the buildings that didn't burn. But the news media creates a powerful impression that all over the country terrible things are happening, that modern life is filled with tragic developments and impending dangers.

Yet this almost certainly doesn't reflect your own day-to-day world. Honestly, is your life filled with life-threatening perils, violence, and extreme need? Or is it one of relative comfort, convenience, and affluence?

A realistic look at your life begins with realizing the truth about your circumstances and the world we live in. Throughout most of human history, physical survival was the overriding problem confronting people. The bulk of each day was spent seeking food, water, shelter, warmth, and safety. Men and women lived lives that were, in Thomas Hobbes's famous phrase, "solitary, poor, nasty, brutish, and short."

Nobody worried about retirement because almost no one lived to be old. By 25, just about everyone was dead, usually of unnatural causes. We battled the elements and hunted and scavenged to survive. As a species, we existed on the brink of starvation in a world filled with danger. Even 200 years ago, well after the advent of agriculture, the vast majority of the world's population experienced the present standard of living of Bangladesh.

Today we have a great bias, a widely accepted belief in the steady nature of progress. Yet for most of human history, there was none. More has been invented in the past 100 years than the previous 1,000. Most of human history has been one prolonged era of non-progress. Gains in living standards were imperceptible. And the human population grew slowly—or not at all—because death rates often exceeded birth rates.

Things improved with the Industrial Revolution. But people worked much harder then than we do today. In 1850, the average workweek was 64 hours. In 1900, it was 53. Today, it is 35 hours. On the whole, Americans work less, have more purchasing power, enjoy goods and services in almost unlimited supply, and have much more leisure time.

One hundred years ago, 6 percent of manufacturing workers took vacations; today, it's over 90 percent. One hundred years ago, the average housekeeper spent 12 hours a day on laundry, cooking, cleaning, and sewing; today's it's about 3 hours.

A century ago, most workers performed backbreaking labor in farming, forestry, construction, or mining. But just a small fraction of the population performs physically demanding work today. That leaves the majority of us free to offer restaurant meals, financial services, jazz concerts, or aromatherapy. Your ancestors a few generations removed would marvel at contemporary life: unlimited food at affordable prices . . . plagues that killed millions—polio, smallpox, measles, rickets—all but eradicated . . . cancer, heart disease, and stroke incidence in decline . . . the advent of instantaneous global communication and same-day travel to distant cities . . . mass home ownership with central heat and air and limitless modern conveniences . . . senior citizens cared for financially and medically, ending the fear of impoverished old age. Thanks to advances in medicine and public safety, we are enjoying the greatest human accomplishment of all time: the near doubling of the average life span over the past 100 years. (At the beginning of the twentieth century, the average American lived just 42 years.) Life expectancy in the West is growing by three months per year. That means you're gaining six hours of life expectancy a day without even exercising. Consequently, the number of years we spend in retirement is increasing, too.

Living standards today are the highest they have ever been, including for the middle class and for the poor. Yes, the median family net worth suffered a hit following the financial crisis of 2008, falling well below the peak of $126,400 in 2007. But with home prices bouncing back and the stock market more than doubling from its lows, prosperity is on the rise again. The Federal Reserve reported in 2013 that American families' wealth had reached an all-time high of $74.8 trillion.

The overwhelming majority of us are seeing our essential needs met and most of our high-priority wants, as well. You may be in the midst of difficult personal circumstances, of course. You may have lost your job, your house, or a loved one. Appreciating this legacy of wealth doesn't require blindness to the tragic aspects of life or the suffering of others. Unlike Dr. Pangloss, I don't believe that everything is for the best in this best of all possible worlds. There are depressing or bittersweet aspects to every life, as there always have been for all people at all times and in all places. Yet if you were born into the affluent West, you live in a world that is vastly richer, easier, and more comfortable than your forebears'.

No doubt you have family problems, or financial troubles or health issues. But people have always dealt with predicaments like these and usually in a milieu much more difficult than our own. A bit of context makes you realize that your life today is almost certainly better than it was for 99.9 percent of your ancestors.

Pessimists grudgingly admit that life may be getting better in some respects, but it is also getting more expensive. And, indeed, inflation is a thief that robs us all. But inflation has been remarkably tame over the last three decades and the real measure of something's worth is the number of hours it takes to acquire it. From this standpoint—again—we have never been richer.

The four most basic human economic needs—food, clothing, fuel, and shelter—have been getting steadily cheaper for years. Housing, for instance, has rarely been a better bargain, and not just because the real estate bubble burst a few years ago. It took 16 weeks to earn the price of 100 square feet of housing in 1956. Today, it takes 14 weeks and the housing is better quality. Plus, our homes are filled with all sorts of modern conveniences: dishwashers, ovens, microwaves, coffee makers, and lounge chairs that give massages.

Most of our grandparents and great grandparents worked long, hard hours to raise lots of kids—thanks to the absence of birth control—in small homes with tiny kitchens and little closet space. The average American home had 1,700 square feet in 1973. Today, it has more than 2,500 square feet, and 40 percent more closet space than in 1978. Today, Americans live in spacious homes with family rooms, pools, and patios, filled with all kinds of desirable things that our grandparents either couldn't have imagined or believed only rich people could own. The average American living under the poverty line today lives in a larger dwelling than the average European. Not the average European living under the poverty line, the average European.

It is easy to take things for granted today. Consider light, for example. To get an hour of artificial light from a sesame-oil lamp in Babylon in 1750 B.C. would have cost you more than 50 hours of work. The same amount of illumination from a tallow candle in the 1800s required 6 hours' labor. Fifteen minutes of work was the trade-off for an hour from a kerosene lamp in the 1880s. Yet for an hour of electric light today, the average American labors *half a second*.

Or take transportation. For millions of years, we got somewhere only by putting one foot in front of the other. Six thousand years ago, we domesticated the horse. (For most of human history, nothing traveled faster than a horse and, as far as we knew, nothing ever would.) In the 1800s, going from New York to Chicago on a stagecoach took two weeks' time and a month's wages. Industrialist Henry Ford made the automobile affordable to the masses a century ago, in any color that you wanted as long as it was black. Today, it takes far less discretionary income for us to buy a car, and—aside from having the power of over 200 horses—the vehicles come with side airbags, antilock brakes, GPS guidance systems, high-powered audio systems, and voice-activated SYNC.

Or consider home entertainment. It just keeps getting better and cheaper. A 50-inch flat screen TV cost more than $10,000 just over a decade ago. Today, you can pick one up at Wal-Mart for less than $500. In 2001, you could spend $600 for a splashy new 1.3-megapixel digital camera that weighed a pound and a half. Today, you can buy a 16-megapixel camera that weighs 3.8 ounces for less than 100 bucks. When DVD players first debuted, they cost several hundred dollars. Today, a good one costs less than $50. Of course, why trouble yourself to buy or rent DVDs when you can easily and cost-efficiently stream content to your home entertainment center without even getting off the couch?

Technology is revolutionizing our lives. Thirty years ago, most people didn't have a personal computer. Twenty years ago, the majority didn't have a cell phone. Ten years ago, most didn't have a high-speed Internet connection. We can't even imagine all the technological advances that lie just ahead.

In 1987, a megabyte of memory cost $5,000. The Mac II that sat on my desk—with a single megabyte of memory and running at 16 megahertz (which Apple in its typically breathless marketing described as "blindingly fast")—cost nearly $6,000. Today, a much smaller and exponentially faster machine costs about a tenth as much. As for memory, you can buy a terabyte drive today for less than 60 bucks. It has never been cheaper to store, exchange, and improve ideas.

In addition to the vast improvement in your material circumstances, you have inherited a tremendously rich cultural legacy: masterpieces of art, music, literature, sculpture, and architecture. And these things have never been more accessible.

Visit any major city and you can marvel at paintings and sculptures that the world's richest men and women cannot own, even if they could afford them. The local library offers all of history's greatest books—with no waiting list. Many can be downloaded for free. Internet radio offers commercial-free music at no cost. And for a few dollars, you can own (and instantly download) high-quality, digital recordings of the world's greatest music performed by the finest symphony orchestras.

Digital music is more environmentally friendly, too. Albums, cassettes, and CDs are made of plastic and metal, the raw ingredients of which have to be extracted from the ground and molded into shape. Unlike digital music, these require packaging. (Older readers will remember early compact disc packaging with jewel cases, plastic wrap, and long cardboard boxes.) And it takes pollution-belching trucks to deliver CDs, records, and tapes to your home. Today, with the exception of greenhouse gases, all forms of pollution are in decline.

In so many ways, you are better off than royalty of yore. Louis XIV lived at Versailles and had cooks and maids and servants waiting on him hand and foot. That sounds great. But he couldn't have imagined our modern conveniences. He lived in a drafty building without central heat in the winter or air-conditioning in the summer.

And what if he got an abscessed tooth or a ruptured appendix? Who would he see? His dinner choices couldn't approach the cornucopia that greets you in a typical supermarket. If he wanted to dine out, he couldn't choose from Italian, Chinese, or Indian cuisine. And today, you can walk into a gas station mini-mart and buy a better wine than he drank.

His Majesty had his own tailors, yes. But he could never have imagined visiting a modern shopping mall or browsing the Internet to order excellent, affordable garments made of silk, linen, cotton, or wool from all over the world. Nor could Louis XIV travel from one town to the next at 70 mph. Or speak to friends or family members in another land. He couldn't fly off to the other side of the world in a matter of hours to enjoy a better climate or an exotic locale for the equivalent of less than $1,000.

Some things, of course, are getting steadily more expensive in real terms. Health care is one of them. But which would you prefer—today's more costly, state-of-the-art health care or what you would have received at a lesser cost in, say, 1975? There has been a stunning reduction in infectious diseases. Heart disease and stroke incidence are in decline. A recent study from the Centers for Disease Control and Prevention reports that overall rates of new cancer diagnosis have dropped steadily since the mid-1990s. (Yet the American Cancer Society reports that 7 in 10 Americans believe cancer rates are going up.)

Today, you can sign up for a hip replacement. Forty years ago you would have gotten a wheelchair. Or maybe you need cataract surgery. A few decades ago you would have gotten a seeing-eye dog. And today's surgery is far less traumatic. Arthroscopic, laparoscopic, endoscopic, drug-eluting stents—these are all commonplace and engineered to get you up and around in no time.

In their book, *Abundance*, technology gurus Peter Diamandis and Steven Kotler describe how rapidly things are improving in our society:

> *Food is cheaper and more plentiful than ever (groceries cost 13 times less today than in 1870). Poverty has declined more in the past 50 years than the previous 500. In fact, adjusted for inflation, incomes have tripled in the past 50 years. Even Americans living under the poverty line today have access to a telephone, toilet, television, running water, air-conditioning, and a car. Go back 150 years and the richest robber barons could have never dreamed of such wealth.*
>
> *Nor are these changes restricted to the developed world. In Africa today a Masai warrior on a cellphone has better mobile communications than the President of the United States did 25 years ago; if he's on a smart phone with Google, he has access to more information than the President did just 15 years ago, with a feast of standard features: watch, stereo, camera, videocamera, voice recorder, GPS tracker, video teleconferencing equipment, a vast library of books, films, games, music. Just 20 years ago these same goods and services would have cost over $1 million . . .*
>
> *Right now all information-based technologies are on exponential growth curves: They're doubling in power for the same price every 12 to*

24 months. This is why an $8 million supercomputer from two decades ago now sits in your pocket and costs less than $200. This same rate of change is also showing up in networks, sensors, cloud computing, 3-D printing, genetics, artificial intelligence, robotics and dozens more industries.

Free markets deliver an enormous bounty based on specialization and exchange. One small example: Our forebears couldn't have conceived today's typical salad bar because they couldn't imagine a global transportation network capable of bringing green beans from Mexico, apples from Poland, and cashews from Vietnam together in the same meal.

The world's poorest are being pulled up, too. Fifty years ago more than half the world's population struggled with getting enough daily calories. Yet predictions that population growth would cause massive food shortages and starvation proved wrong. Genetically modified seeds allow farmers to produce better-quality crops while using fewer pesticides, herbicides, and fertilizers. The sustainability of the land has improved as a result. America's farmers now grow five times as much corn as they did in the 1930s— on 20 percent less land. The yield per acre has grown sixfold in the past 70 years.

The poor are actually experiencing the most dramatic rise in living standards. According to UNICEF, the global infant mortality rate is the lowest it has ever been, at 51 deaths per 1,000 live births. Child labor, while still too high, is a tenth of what it was five decades ago. The daily calorie intake in the developing world is up dramatically. There are roughly seven billion people in the world, but virtually everywhere health is improving and life expectancy is up.

At the current rate of decline, the number of people in the world living in "absolute poverty" will be statistically insignificant by 2035. The spread of microfinance and cell phone technology in many developing countries, for example, is creating countless opportunities and greater prosperity.

The overwhelming majority of us are far better fed, sheltered, entertained, and protected against disease than our grandparents. Plus, the majority of our ancestors enjoyed virtually none of the political freedoms we take for granted in the West today: freedom of speech, freedom of assembly, freedom of religion, freedom from conscription, freedom to choose our leaders or to pursue our economic self-interest.

Educational attainment has never been higher. Eighty-eight percent of Americans are high school graduates. Over 57 percent have some college. And 40 percent have a bachelor's degree. Yes, the cost of higher education has been growing faster than the rate of inflation, but there are signs this is changing, too. Online universities are revolutionizing higher education. And almost two-thirds of colleges now offer full online degree programs, nearly double what it was 10 years ago. And if knowledge rather than a degree is your goal, high-quality courses—from Kahn Academy to Coursera—are available online and absolutely free.

IQ scores are rising as well. In fact, the average has risen by 15 points in the last 50 years in the United States. That means a person with an average IQ of 100 today would score 115 on a test from the 1960s.

Throughout most of American history, many groups were systematically marginalized. But formal discrimination against women and minorities has ended. Gays and lesbians are next. Polls show the majority of Americans now favor full and equal rights for homosexual couples.

Walter Isaacson, former managing editor of *Time*, once noted that if you had to describe the twentieth century's geopolitics in one sentence, it could be a short one: Freedom won. Free minds and free markets prevailed over fascism and communism.

The world is getting steadily safer, too. Although you wouldn't know it listening to your local TV station, crime is in a long-term cycle of decline.

This is the most peaceable era in the history of our species. The number of people who have died as a result of war, civil war, and terrorism is down 50 percent this decade from the 1990s. It is down 75 percent from the preceding five decades. And this greater stability has allowed the creation of a single global economic system, in which countries around the world are participating and flourishing.

There is too much conflict, especially in the Middle East and parts of Africa. But this is newsworthy, in part, because it is increasingly rare. In his essay "A History of Violence," Harvard psychologist Steven Pinker writes:

> *Cruelty as entertainment, human sacrifice to indulge superstition, slavery as a labor-saving device, conquest as the mission statement of government, genocide as a means of acquiring real estate, torture and mutilation as routine punishment, the death penalty for misdemeanors and differences of opinion, assassination as the mechanism of political succession, rape as the spoils of war, pogroms as outlets for frustration, homicide as the major form of conflict resolution—all were unexceptionable features of life for most of human history. But, today, they are rare to nonexistent in the West, far less common elsewhere than they used to be, and widely condemned when they are brought to light."*

Never before has the risk of death by violence been smaller for most of humanity. Yes, there are armed conflicts around the globe, but the richest countries are not in geopolitical competition with one another, fighting proxy wars, or engaging in arms races. This is huge. There is a fundamental difference between growing up knowing your existence is precarious and growing up feeling that your survival is secure. This leads not just to material security but to a feeling of subjective well-being.

I don't mean to downplay our current challenges, including one of the most predictable crises in the nation's history: huge and growing state and federal deficits. Yet you'll notice that the extreme forecasts always begin with the words "If nothing is done . . ."

Yet something *will* be done. Only the most hardened cynics believe that politics will ultimately trump the national welfare. The solutions are not politically easy, but they exist. Simpson-Bowles and other bipartisan commissions have already delineated the steps necessary to reach fiscal sanity. State governors like Chris Christie and Andrew Cuomo have tackled deeply entrenched problems, such as pension shortfalls, that threaten to destroy state budgets. There is political polarization and plenty of heated rhetoric, but reform at the national level is coming. Yes, it is overdue, but this is hardly new. Winston Churchill was right when he observed that Americans can always be counted on to do the right thing after they have exhausted all the other possibilities.

In sum, the world you live in is rich by almost every measure. Your circumstances are not just fortuitous but extraordinary. We should all recognize this and remember it. Human beings have never had it so good. Our lives are bountiful beyond measure. Yet Americans don't report being any more satisfied today than they did in the 1940s when we were in the fight of our lives against Hitler, Mussolini, and Hirohito.

It's not uncommon to hear people grumble because they can't get a high-speed Internet connection on the plane, or that Web pages are taking too long to load on their smartphone, or the supermarket is out of their favorite gourmet pet food. As essayist Randall Jarrell observed: "People who live in a Golden Age usually go around complaining how yellow everything looks."

There is a serious downside to all this gloom and doom. For starters, despite the many positive developments in society, diagnoses of clinical depression are up 10-fold in the past 50 years. Some of this is due to the increasing willingness of those afflicted to seek treatment. But surely environmental factors contribute as well. And what could be more depressing than the daily drumbeat of pessimism—and an almost complete absence of positive news—from major media sources? Even among those who enjoy robust mental health, all this negativity—in addition to distorting our perspective—is, to put it mildly, "a bummer."

I also see serious ramifications in my bailiwick, the investment arena. Entrepreneurs who don't feel optimistic about the future don't start new businesses or expand existing ones. Investors don't risk their money in the stock market—and thereby decrease their chances of meeting their investment goals. That delays retirement or diminishes your future standard of living.

Over the past 15 years, we have had real booms and busts. But they have also been peppered with false alarms: Y2K, acid rain, natural resource depletion, mineral shortages, the bird flu epidemic, government shutdown threats, and "the sequester." Yet if you adopt an optimistic attitude you may be branded naïve or out of touch. As the Austrian economist Friedrich Hayek said, "Implicit confidence in the beneficence of progress has come to be regarded as the sign of a shallow mind."

Most people—even scientists and sociologists—fail to recognize the incredible power of dynamic change. Human beings, technology, and capital markets now operate as a collective problem-solving machine. When a resource becomes scarce, for example, it drives up the price. That encourages both conservation and the development of alternatives and efficiencies. When whales grew scarce, for example, petroleum was used instead as a source of oil. (There should be a poster of John D. Rockefeller hanging in every Greenpeace office.) And when oil prices spiked recently, factories, utilities, and truck manufacturers switched from oil to cheaper, cleaner natural gas.

We underestimate the power of human ingenuity and the incentives that society provides for problem solvers. Instead we tend to focus on the daily white noise of setbacks, problems and negative developments, missing the big story in the process.

In this book, I intend to share a particular perspective. Whatever problems you are grappling with, whatever may be wrong in your life, it can only be improved by recognizing that you are heir to an enormously rich social, political, economic, scientific, technological and cultural legacy, a true embarrassment of riches.

In countless ways—both large and small—we are among the most fortunate people who have ever lived. The essays that follow are one man's attempt to prove it.

PART ONE

A WEALTH OF GRATITUDE

Imagine walking into a room full of strangers and searching in vain to find some commonality. The folks there have various educational backgrounds and vocations, represents different age groups, races and creeds, and hale from different parts of the country.

Then you discover something odd. Everyone in the room is a lottery winner. Would that not be an astonishing coincidence? Of course it would. Yet you and everyone you know have already beaten longer odds than any Powerball winner. You just don't realize it.

For example, when you consider your good fortune, you probably tell yourself something like, "I have decent health, a loving family, good friends, a comfortable home, and plenty of stuff."

Yet, important as these things are, it hardly scratches the surface. The very fact that you are here at all would defy the odds–makers. In "Unweaving the Rainbow," Oxford biologist Richard Dawkins puts things in perspective:

"We are going to die, and that makes us the lucky ones. Most people are never going to die because they are never going to be born. The potential people who could have been here in my place but who will in fact never see the light of day outnumber the sand grains of Sahara. Certainly those unborn ghosts include greater poets than Keats, scientists greater than Newton. We know this because the set of possible people allowed by our DNA so massively outnumbers the set of actual people. In the teeth of these stupefying odds it is you and I, in our ordinariness, that are here."

Consider how little chance you had of ever arriving at this party. Every one of your forebears had to be attractive enough to find a mate, healthy enough to reproduce, and sufficiently blessed by fate and circumstances to live long enough to do so. Each was able to deliver a tiny charge of genetic material to the right partner at the right moment in order to perpetuate the only possible sequence of hereditary combinations that would result in you.

The chances of your ever being born are almost incalculably slim. The odds against arriving in the modern era are also staggering. And you were likely born in the prosperous West. Billions alive today were born into wrenching poverty in China, India, sub-Saharan Africa, or some miserable failed state.

You could easily be living in a society without Western freedoms, modern infrastructure, or even a reliable power supply. You might have no free-market system to incentivize you, no police force to protect you, no reliable court system to enforce contracts or protect your rights.

Recognize that, whatever your personal circumstances, you have been astoundingly fortunate. Why is this important to know? Because it puts things in perspective. We should all feel immense appreciation for the life that we were given—and make a conscious effort to practice looking at what's right in our lives rather than what's missing.

As Cicero noted a couple thousand years ago, "Gratitude is not only the greatest of virtues, but the parent of all the others."

A Message from the Land of the Unwell

While sitting at home one spring evening in 2013, I suddenly began getting sharp, stabbing pains in what I thought was my stomach. I couldn't even stand up. And the pains didn't go away. They got worse.

After 30 minutes of agony, my wife, Karen, insisted we were going to the emergency room. I didn't object.

After four hours of poking, prodding, X-rays, and CAT scans, I got the news. My stomach was fine. But my large intestine was a train wreck. I had a volvulus. That's fancy talk for an intestine that looks like a pretzel twist. How it got that way is a bit of a mystery, but the condition requires immediate intervention as a lack of blood flow can cause tissue death, not to mention the big event itself.

The on-call surgeon—who said she'd never seen a case as severe as mine (comforting)—said the situation was dire. And while she couldn't be sure until she got in there and started nosing around, the CAT scans also indicated I had a tumor.

Great.

There wasn't time for a lot of deliberation. A medical team prepped me for surgery and had me sign the usual boilerplate acknowledging the potential dangers and complications, including leaving the operating room with the bed sheet over my nose instead of under it. I scribbled my name.

When I came to in the recovery room a few hours later, I had the distinct feeling someone had machine-gunned me in the gut. But I was too woozy to care. After a few groggy minutes, an orderly wheeled me into a post-op room with various tubes sticking in me or extruding out, none of them particularly pleasant.

The next few days were a combination of agony and tedium. Being hooked up to a gaggle of machines in a small, windowless room and surviving on hospital broth and saline solution doesn't lend itself to poetry.

"Press this button and your IV will release pain medication," the nurse told me. "Hit it as often as you feel you need it. But it won't release a dose more than once every six minutes."

I nodded and pressed the button.

How did this happen? One minute I'm sitting at home wondering whether there was anything less stupid on TV. The next I'm strapped to a gurney with tubes up my nose and in my arm, with a scar on my belly that would make Dr. Frankenstein proud.

After a brief assessment, however, I noted a few positives. First, there was no tumor. (Hallelujah.) Second, the attack didn't come in the middle of my recent trips to Laos, Cambodia, or Vietnam. Or during one of my solo hikes in the Blue Ridge Mountains. Or at 30,000 feet. In short, thanks to the prompt attention I received, I was still on the right side of the daisies.

I had a few other epiphanies as well. The biggest is that you cannot adequately appreciate what nurses do until you are under their care. They are truly angels on earth. How does someone spend their days trafficking in blood, bile, vomit, phlegm, sweat, pus, and other human excreta while fluffing pillows, maintaining a cheery disposition, and exhibiting a sincere desire to make you feel as comfortable as possible? I'm not cut out for that kind of work myself. (Of course, you probably don't want your nurse giving you investment advice either, but it takes about a nanosecond to determine who is expendable here.)

The next realization I had was how much friends and family mean at times like these. Under ordinary circumstances, these are the folks you laugh with, play with, kvetch with. But when you are flat on your back and tethered to the blinking, beeping gray towers that crowd your bed, they are your lifeline to sanity. Never wonder whether a card, a call, or a visit is worth the trouble. It is.

I was also surprised to see how easy it is to adopt a covetous spirit. As I hobbled down the hallway in my ward, hunched over and leaning on my nurse, who was pulling the IV stand, I looked with awe and envy at the hospital visitors passing by. "Look at them," I thought. "Shoulders back, arms swinging freely, no pain whatsoever. How lucky to be *them*."

Of course, this ridiculous attitude gets quashed in a hurry when the hospital PA booms out—as it does every few hours: "*Code Blue. Special teams report to Room 223 immediately. Code Blue. Special teams to Room 223.*" You may think things are tough. But there are always people going through worse.

And not just inside the hospital. While I was there, for instance, my old friend Rob learned that his wife, Laura, had breast cancer and needed a mastectomy. My close friend and neighbor, Katy, watched her mother suffer a massive stroke just weeks after starting chemotherapy. She died a few days later, becoming the fourth cancer victim in her family in four years. Sometimes you wonder how much heartbreak a single household can endure.

Being in the hospital also gave me a renewed appreciation of the power of science and medicine. Throughout 99.9 percent of human history, people who developed my particular gastrointestinal problem had a common experience. They died. We are incredibly fortunate to be among the tiny fraction of 1 percent of humanity who live in an era of scientific understanding, medical know-how, and—never underestimate it—general anesthesia.

So what causes cecal volvulus? That's what friends and family members kept asking me all week. The scary part is that doctors really don't know. You do get more susceptible as you get older, so Baby Boomers like me are hearing more about it. As my friend Jimmy commented in the hospital, "Colonic volvulus? Oh, right. I had two dogs and a horse that died from that."

He almost added a buddy to that list. After the operation, my surgeon said my situation was so extreme that I may have been less than 24 hours from a catastrophic bursting of the intestine.

That isn't how I ever imagined things would end. I always thought I might go quietly in my sleep, like my grandfather did. Not yelling and screaming like the passengers in his car. (Terrible joke, I know.)

The next week a friend asked me if these events shook me up, changed me. I wouldn't pass a polygraph if I said the experience wasn't a bit unsettling. But my recovery went well. There was no postoperative infection and I gradually weaned myself off the painkillers.

As for any lasting change, probably not. Within a few days I was back home, annoying everyone the same as before, but this time with a heightened realization that you may have personal problems, you may have family problems or career problems or financial problems, but if you or someone you love doesn't have a major medical problem—believe me—things could be worse.

THE REASON YOU
SHOULD BE BIASED

I'm sometimes accused of being overly optimistic. Mea culpa. I *am* an optimist, always have been. Every project I undertake, I expect to see to a successful conclusion. When events take a turn for the worse, I start imagining how they will get better. My general attitude is that things will work out, even though—needless to say—sometimes they don't.

We all walk around carrying mental images of what the world is like and how the future will unfold. Some see the glass as half full. Others don't. Yet psychologists have discovered that the vast majority of healthy, successful individuals are optimistic, even when it isn't warranted. It turns out many of us truly are wearing rose-colored glasses. And it helps.

Cognitive scientists reveal that this illusion serves an important function: it turns possibilities into probabilities. Moreover, there is mounting evidence that those who take a pessimistic attitude—even if they are sometimes correct—are risking their careers, their personal relationships, and even *their health*.

Neuroscientist Tali Sharot writes in *The Optimism Bias: A Tour of the Irrationally Positive Brain*:

> The data clearly shows that most people overestimate their pros-
> pects for professional achievement; expect their children to be

extraordinarily gifted; miscalculate their likely life span (sometimes by twenty years or more); expect to be healthier than the average person and more successful than their peers; hugely underestimate the likelihood of divorce, cancer and unemployment; and are confident overall that their future lives will be better than those their parents put up with. This is known as the optimism bias—the inclination to overestimate the likelihood of encountering positive events in the future and to underestimate the likelihood of experiencing negative events.

Studies show that large majorities of us believe we are smarter, friendlier, more honest, and better looking than the average person. (And better drivers!) This, of course, is impossible. *Most* people cannot be better than *most* people. (Yet we are generally just as blind to this *superiority illusion* as we are to our optimism bias.)

However, this self-deception is not only healthy but invaluable. Optimism evokes new behavior that often creates a self-fulfilling prophecy.

Take the example of two middle-aged men—one an optimist, the other a pessimist—who find themselves in the emergency room following a heart attack. Other factors being equal, the optimist has a better chance of a full recovery, not because positive thinking itself changes his prognosis but because it leads to favorable changes in his behavior. The pessimist feels resigned. But the optimist is more likely to stop smoking, avoid fatty foods and salt, engage in moderate exercise, and avoid stress-inducing situations. It's this change in his actions—not the sunny outlook itself—that improves his chances.

Research shows that when we alter our perceptions and dreams about the future in positive ways, it reduces anxiety and improves physical and mental health. It also motivates us to be proactive. That's because human brains have a strong propensity to transform what we imagine into reality. Optimistic beliefs, even if they are unjustified, are often the precursor to positive actions.

This is particularly important when it comes to running your portfolio. In my experience, successful stock market investors have an optimistic long-term view that simply doesn't have an off switch. That doesn't mean we don't hedge our bets or take concrete steps to reduce risk and volatility. We do. But we also tend to have an abiding faith in the ability of entrepreneurs, businesses, and capital markets to succeed in meeting people's economic needs.

In the depths of the financial meltdown in 2008, for example, Warren Buffett penned an op-ed piece for the *New York Times* in which he encouraged investors to snap out of their funk:

> Today people who hold cash equivalents feel comfortable. They shouldn't. They have opted for a terrible long-term asset, one that pays virtually nothing and will only depreciate in value. Equities will almost certainly outperform cash over the next decade, probably by a substantial degree. . . . Most major companies will be setting new profit records 5, 10 and 20 years from now.

At the time, I agreed with his general assessment. But with the storm clouds gathering—and Wall Street titans falling like flies—I thought his forecast that American corporations would report record profits in five years was insanely optimistic. I was wrong. And so was Buffett. The companies that make up the Standard & Poor's (S&P) 500 were earning all-time record profits just 18 months later. And they hit new records every quarter for the next four years.

Of course, optimism alone—wishful thinking—doesn't change much. And sometimes circumstances are entirely outside our control. For example, it really didn't matter whether passengers aboard the *Titanic* were looking forward to a relaxing ocean voyage.

But in some situations, optimism is the key difference. Here's why: When you expect a positive outcome and it doesn't happen, the frontal lobes of your brain go into overdrive, frantically trying to figure out what went wrong and how to make the necessary adjustments. But when you expect a negative outcome, setbacks create no surprise or conflict in the brain. Changes and improvements aren't forthcoming because failure was already anticipated.

Studies show that pessimism promotes passivity and hopelessness. Research by Martin Seligman, a pioneer in the field of positive psychology, demonstrates that pessimists often behave helplessly, harming their chances of achieving desirable results and even feeding depression.

Other people, too, are hugely affected by the expectations you place on them. Employees are more productive when you expect excellence and industry. Students do better when teachers believe they are exceptional, even when they aren't.

When the Lakers beat the Celtics in the 1987 NBA championship, coach Pat Riley didn't just predict the team would win again the next year; he offered Laker fans and the world his *personal guarantee*. In an interview, Magic Johnson said, "Of all the psychological things that Pat's come up with, this is probably the best." Teammates showed up at camp believing their coach's credibility was on the line. The Lakers did win again. And when a reporter asked Riley during the victory celebration if he could guarantee a third consecutive championship, Kareem Abdul-Jabbar jumped up to cover his mouth. He later explained that he couldn't take another year of that kind of pressure.

Optimism doesn't mean we turn a blind eye to negative circumstances or we never entertain darker thoughts. But, more than we realize, our expectations influence both our perception of reality and our actions, and so alter reality itself.

There is a huge payoff in seeing gray skies as just passing clouds. Optimists expect to have meaningful relationships; good health; and happy, productive lives. They live longer, make better financial plans, and despair and worry less. They avoid needless anxiety and adjust better to stress.

Optimism is a source of vitality and hope, courage, and confidence. It motivates us to set goals, to take risks. It encourages persistence in the face of obstacles. As Winston Churchill said, "For myself, I am an optimist—it does not seem to be much use being anything else."

◼ WHAT WE LIVE TO DISCOVER

On a recent trip to Italy, I visited the Sistine Chapel again and gazed at the ceiling until my neck hurt. It is truly one of the world's most astonishing works of art.

Some would go even further, calling Michelangelo's famous fresco—a synthesis of biblical history before the advent of Christ—one of the highest pinnacles of creative achievement, perhaps the single greatest painting in the history of Western civilization.

Superlatives like these are impossible to justify, of course. But we tend to wax poetic when the subject is beauty—a tough quality to analyze or even define. Yet few doubt its importance. As the Arabic poet Kahlil Gibran observed, "We live only to discover beauty. All else is a form of waiting."

When we're young, of course, we're cautioned against superficial judgments. We're warned that beauty is in the eye of the beholder, that it is only skin deep, and that we can't judge a book by its cover. All true. Yet deep inside, most of us imagine ourselves connoisseurs of beauty, that we have an eye for it.

What is the beautiful, exactly? The Italian Renaissance artist Alberti described it as that from which nothing can be taken away and to which nothing can be added except for the worse. He saw beauty as the approach to perfection. And I think that's about right. Consider Shakespeare's plays, Monet's *Water Lilies*, Bach's two- and three-part inventions, or Keira Knightley's face. It's hard to imagine any improvements.

Beauty compels us to stop, notice, and admire. Enter a home with elegant furnishings, attractive art, colorful arrangements, or a breathtaking view, and we immediately fall under its spell. The experience often encourages us to reevaluate our own situation and perhaps change the quality of our poorly improvised lives.

Wherever we go, beauty doesn't just attract attention. It demands it. Only those who don't perceive it can be indifferent to it. Our species's preoccupation with beauty is everywhere apparent. Most of us prefer to live in lovely surroundings with attractive mates, stylish clothes, and beautiful objects. Note as well our love of natural settings, our devotion to the arts, our culture's obsession with youth.

The appreciation of beauty is as old as humanity itself. The ancients revered it. Classical sculptures portrayed ideal human forms. Renaissance architecture was all about harmony, symmetry, and proportionality. In "Ode on a Grecian Urn," John Keats even equated beauty with truth, claiming that was all we could know or needed to know.

Scholar Roger Scruton thinks he understands why:

> Beauty is an ultimate value—something that we pursue for its own sake. . . . [It] should therefore be compared to truth and goodness, one member of a trio of ultimate values which justify our rational inclinations. Why believe p? Because it is true. Why want x? Because it is good. Why look at y? Because it is beautiful.

Beauty is a universal value. Around the world and through the ages, there have been cultures without math, language, technology, or medicine, but none without art, from the earliest drawings in the Lascaux caves to Beethoven's symphonies to Frank Lloyd Wright's creations. Of course, a thing needn't reach these levels of magnificence. There is everyday beauty in a manicured lawn, an elegant shirt, or a well-set dinner table.

The importance we attach to beauty is clear in the language we use to describe it. The painting is *dazzling*. The sunrise is *awe-inspiring*. The bride is *radiant*. Many of the world's greatest masterworks are described as *ravishing*. They fill us with wonder, reverence, or delight. We may even refer to their *sheer beauty*, warning listeners that words won't convey our sense of rapture.

Beauty has an inviting quality (something restaurant proprietors clearly understand, judging by the number of attractive young women employed at hostess stands). Filmmakers make sure the good guys are hunks. The bad guys, by comparison, sport bad haircuts, uneven teeth, and prominent scars. There is no easier way to deceive an audience than to reveal that the handsome hero or heroine is the real villain.

In our collective conscience, good looks are often equated with honesty and goodness (even though in real life great beauty and great virtue rarely go hand in hand). Our bias is so widely recognized that there is even a term for it: *lookism*. The word is used to describe preferential treatment based on a person's physical appearance. Indeed, studies show that a preference for beautiful faces emerges early in child development and that physically attractive adults tend to have more friends, better social skills, and even higher incomes.

Evolutionary psychologists argue that our sense of beauty emerged, in part, through the process of sexual selection. Men and women, while certainly giving consideration to other qualities, are everywhere drawn to regular features and well-proportioned bodies. This aesthetic appeal exists even in the animal kingdom. In *The Descent of Man*, Charles Darwin pointed out that the peacock's large and magnificent tail both attracts predators and makes him less able to flee. Yet it does provide one clear evolutionary advantage. Potential mates prefer it. To peahens, apparently, *size matters*.

Nature is filled with countless examples of beauty. One of life's great surprises is how the natural world—with its blue skies, green foliage, and orange and purple sunsets—is far more gorgeous than it needs to be. There are good reasons for this, of course. Chorophyll gives plants their green color. The sky and sea are blue because of the diffraction of light. And at twilight, rays of sunlight pass through more of the Earth's atmosphere before reaching us, creating glorious sunrises and sunsets. Still, nature could be far dowdier and just as fruitful.

A thing needn't be inspiring or uplifting to be beautiful, of course. Some of the greatest works of art are devoted to the real and unpleasant truth of our condition. One of my favorite pieces of orchestral music, for instance, is Rachmaninoff's *Isle of the Dead*, a relentlessly dark and forbidding piece that is also deeply moving. The same is true of downbeat movies like *The Deer Hunter* or *The Passion of the Christ* and classic novels like *Lolita* or *Jude the Obscure*.

In sum, beauty reminds us of the worthwhileness of life. Our days can be filled with mundane thoughts, utilitarian calculations, and constant striving. Beauty provides a respite, as welcome as a cold glass of water on an August afternoon.

In a world of resentment, envy, and mistrust, beauty jolts us out of our cynicism and complacency and reminds us of our harmony with nature and with each other. It breaks monotony and reminds us of important truths: the resplendence of nature, the loveliness of youth, the ephemerality of life.

Beauty is a doorway to the transcendental. (Duck into almost any cathedral and you'll see.) It delights and refreshes us, asking us to find meaning, make critical comparisons, and examine our way of living.

There is truth in Oscar Wilde's quip that it is only a shallow person who does not judge by appearances. To be blind to beauty is to be blind to life.

Or, at least, some of the most attractive parts of it.

LIKE NO OTHER NATION IN THE WORLD

Of all the arguments during the 2012 presidential election, perhaps none was sillier than the left/right debate about whether America is an exceptional nation.

As every schoolchild knows, the founding of the United States was *revolutionary*—not in the sense of replacing one set of rulers with another, but in placing political authority in the hands of the people. It is the only nation in the world founded on the equality of men, individual freedom, and the rule of law. Our Declaration of Independence is a timeless statement of inherent rights, the proper purposes of government, and the limits of political authority. Our core beliefs are enshrined in the Constitution and Bill of Rights, the longest-serving foundation of liberty in history.

Our principles ensure that everyone has the right to the fruits of their own labor. The fundamental right to acquire, possess, and sell property is the backbone of opportunity and the most practical means to pursue human happiness. Our free enterprise system is the source of prosperity and the foundation of economic liberty.

The U.S. economy produces almost a quarter of the world's wealth. The Internet was created here. And so were great innovative companies like Apple, Amazon, Facebook, and Google. Why weren't they founded in other wealthy industrial nations with large, well-educated, and hard-working populations? One reason is that the United States is the most meritocratic nation on earth. No one needs to hail from the right family, be the right age, or have the right connections to get a fair shake. There are no class distinctions, no caste system.

The U.S. military is the primary defender of the free world. Our government plays an extraordinary role in world leadership. And the American people are the most affluent and charitable in the world.

Yet *Washington Post* columnist Richard Cohen calls American exceptionalism a "myth" and insists that we should junk a phrase "that reeks of arrogance" and narcissism. Political commentator Michael Kinsley similarly mocked the idea in an essay for *Politico*, calling the very notion a "conceit." Even President Obama seemed to equivocate. Asked early in his presidency whether he believed in American exceptionalism, he replied, "I believe in American exceptionalism, just as I suspect that the Brits believe in British exceptionalism and the Greeks believe in Greek exceptionalism."

Love of homeland is universal, of course. Yet the Frenchman Alexis de Tocqueville observed something distinctly different about us as far back as the 1830s. He noted that Americans pursue their economic interests with passion, but also enthusiastically form associations to take up public affairs and tend to the needs of their communities.

Social scientist Charles Murray writes:

Historically, Americans have been different as a people, even peculiar, and everyone around the world has recognized it. I'm thinking of qualities such as American optimism even when there doesn't seem to be any good reason for it. That's quite uncommon among the peoples of the world. There is the striking lack of class envy in America—by and large, Americans celebrate others' success instead of resenting it. And then there is perhaps the most important symptom of all, the signature of American exceptionalism— the assumption by most Americans that they are in control of their own destinies. It is hard to think of a more inspiriting quality for a population to possess, and the American population still possesses it to an astonishing degree. No other country comes close.

Our nation's growth and prosperity have been extraordinary. How did our small republican experiment transform and dominate global culture and society? Geography played a big role. Buffered by two oceans and a rugged frontier, we had plenty of cheap land and vast natural resources. (But then so did countries like Russia and Brazil.) Entrepreneurs were also given free license to innovate and create. Profit was never something to apologize for. Rather, it was viewed as proof that the businessman offered customers something more valuable than the money they traded.

We also opened our arms to tens of millions of immigrants who dreamed of a better life and helped to build this country. In the process, we developed an astounding capacity for tolerance. Today, we live peaceably alongside each other, unperturbed by differences of religion or ethnicity. Compare this to Europe's tragic history of massacres, pogroms, population transfers, and genocides.

Not that we don't have blemishes. At our country's birth, Native Americans were ruthlessly subjugated, millions of blacks were held in slavery, and only white men with property were allowed to vote or hold office. In the years afterward, we discriminated against minorities, fought senseless wars, meddled needlessly in other countries' affairs, and incarcerated an extraordinary percentage of our citizens.

Still, America is not just a nation but an *ideal*. We may fall short of it, but we keep striving to fulfill that vision, to embody our founding creed of liberty, justice, and equality.

More than two centuries after the American Revolution, the principles proclaimed in the Declaration of Independence and promulgated by the Constitution still define us as a nation. These permanent truths are not just for us but, as Abraham Lincoln said, "applicable to all men and all times."

I'm not suggesting that other nations don't have proud histories, unique traditions, or beautiful cultures. I am delighted when I get a chance to visit Shanghai or Buenos Aires, not to mention Rome or Paris. There's a lot to love about day-to-day life in other countries.

But people around the globe don't talk about the French Dream or the Chinese Dream. Only one nation is universally recognized as the Land of Opportunity. Only one country attracts more students, more immigrants, and more investment capital than any other.

Why? Because America cultivates, celebrates, and rewards the habits that make men and women successful. Our free, merit-based society promises that anyone with ambition and grit can move up the economic ladder, that everyone has a chance to better his or her lot, regardless of circumstances.

In short, the American Revolution laid out the universal principles of freedom. The Declaration of Independence holds that all people everywhere are endowed with the right to liberty and that governments are legitimate only if they derive their just powers from the consent of the governed.

The notion that America is something very special is *not*, as some would argue, just a crude strain of patriotism. The United States embodies timeless ideals, an optimistic attitude, a can-do spirit, and an enthusiastic endorsement of the pursuit of happiness through individual initiative and self-reliance. In this sense—among others—we are *truly* an exceptional nation.

How to Put a Touch of Glory in Your Life

There's an old story about a man who walks by a construction site and sees workmen pushing wheelbarrows, each filled with an enormous stone. He asks one of the men what they're doing.

"What does it look like?" he answers with a sneer. "We're hauling rocks."

That hardly satisfies the man's curiosity, so he asks another construction worker the same question. The workman doesn't bother looking up. "We're putting up a wall."

Still frustrated, the man tries one last time. "I say there," he asks the next worker, "can you tell me what you men are doing here?"

The workman puts down his wheelbarrow, wipes his forehead, and says with a broad smile, "We're building a cathedral."

Here are three men, all doing the same job. One is hauling rocks. One is putting up a wall. One is building a cathedral. This story says a lot about the attitude we bring to our lives—or could if we were willing to adjust our perspective.

My primary occupation, for example, is writing investment advice. One reason I write is to meet my overhead. To that extent, I'm hauling rocks. A greater objective is to help build a publishing business. The more paying readers we attract and the better we market ourselves, the faster our bottom line grows. To that extent, I'm putting up walls.

But the real objective of my writing is to help readers achieve and maintain financial independence. When I stay focused on that, I'm building a cathedral. (And, not incidentally, meeting my lesser goals as well.) Idealists might counter that creating wealth has nothing to do with building cathedrals. But they are sorely mistaken.

You can improve yourself, voice your opinions, or organize around a cause without cash. But you won't affect much change in your community—or build an actual cathedral—without it. Contrary to what some believe, money isn't about having "more stuff." Money is independence. It liberates you from want, from work that is drudgery, from relationships that confine you. You can't reach your potential or live life to the fullest if you spend your days swimming in concerns about money. No one is truly free who is a slave to his job, his creditors, his circumstances, or his overhead.

Wealth is the great equalizer. It doesn't matter if you're a man or woman, black or white, young or old, handsome or homely, gay or straight, educated or not. If you have money, you have power . . . in the best sense.

Wealth is freedom, security, and peace of mind. It allows you to help others, to do and be what you want. It enables you to follow your dreams, to spend your life the way *you* choose. Money gives you dignity. It gives you choices. That's why every man and woman has the right—perhaps even the responsibility—to pursue some level of financial freedom, whether you define that as being independently wealthy or just climbing out from under your credit card debt. When my investment advice empowers people, when it gives them security or peace of mind, I feel good about my work. I'm building a cathedral.

You can apply the same line of thinking to whatever you do. My friend John Mackey, for instance, is the founder and CEO of Whole Foods, the world's largest chain of natural and organic food stores. It is his responsibility to oversee and grow a $19 billion corporation. In my conversations with him, however, I find that what *really* excites him is showing people how to enjoy longer, healthier, more disease-resistant lives. His firm has even launched Wellness Clubs within its stores to educate customers and offer them free classes on nutrition, diet, and healthier cooking.

Will this also help Whole Foods increase its profits? I don't see how it couldn't. But to the extent that John and his team are helping people live longer, healthier lives, they are also building cathedrals.

Want to put a touch of glory in your life? Find a way to tweak your perspective, to understand how what you do—in your home, in the workplace, or for a nonprofit organization—meets other people's needs or improves their lives.

In the end, we all have a choice. You can haul rocks. You can put up walls. Or you can build a cathedral.

THE GREATEST STAR OF THEM ALL

Familiarity can be the enemy of awe and wonder. This is particularly true of our sun. Throughout most of human history, we had no idea that it was a star . . . or that the stars scattered across the night sky were other suns unimaginably far away.

For thousands of years, it was an article of faith that the world was an immovable disk around which the sun, the planets, and the stars all revolved. Everyone believed, indeed, *knew* this.

That changed only a few centuries ago. And it is only within the last few decades—using everything from ground-based telescopes and spectroscopes to the space-based Solar & Heliospheric Observatory (SOHO)—that we gained a real understanding of our powerful neighbor. So let's take a closer look at the celestial giant on which so much of our lives depends. . . .

The sun is 93 million miles away. A passenger jet flying 550 miles per hour would take 20 years to get there. To reach the next nearest star, Alpha Centauri, that same plane would need five million years.

The sun is by far the largest object in our neighborhood, making up 99.8 percent of the mass of the solar system. Its diameter is 865,000 miles. Were it hollow, 1.3 million earths could fit inside it. Yet, in astronomical terms, the sun is just an average-sized gas ball out of some 200 billion in the Milky Way galaxy.

Things look fairly placid here on Earth, if not downright stationary. But that is an illusion, of course. The Earth spins on its axis at 1,040 miles an hour while chugging around the sun at 66,600 miles per hour. Meanwhile, the sun, with its retinue of planets, is screaming around the center of the galaxy at 483,000 miles per hour while the Milky Way itself moves toward the Andromeda galaxy at a hair-raising 1.3 million miles per hour.

The sun is the most alien place in the solar system. Its interior is unimaginably hot—at 27 million degrees Fahrenheit—and converts 400 million tons of hydrogen into helium every second. Indeed, conditions there are so extreme that hydrogen and helium atoms break into their constituent parts, protons and electrons, and re-fuse into heavier elements. That process, called nuclear fusion, is what makes stars shine. Author and astronomer Bob Berman writes, "The power of the sun's continuous nuclear fusion is equal to 91 billion megatons of TNT per second. That's 91 billion standard one-megaton H-bombs going off in the time it takes to say 'Holy moly.'"

Fortunately, we're a safe distance away. In fact, we're the perfect distance away. Venus is a boiling mess. Mars is a frozen desert. But you and I are here because we inhabit "the Goldilocks zone," a region where temperatures are moderate and water can exist as a liquid.

We are all tied to the sun in the most intimate ways. It is the master timekeeper, marking off our days and nights as well as the years. The sun drives our weather and climate and even affects your moods.

Psychologists are familiar with something called seasonal affective disorder (SAD). When the skies turn gray, the weather cools, and the days shorten, our bodies slow down, our energy wanes, and our outlook darkens. Your biological clock and even your disposition are affected by sunlight (or the lack of it). And we need this precious resource to live. True, too much sunlight is damaging. But too little is dangerous, too. Sun rays generate vitamin D, a substance that strengthens your immune system, protects against rickets, and combats osteoporosis, multiple sclerosis, rheumatoid arthritis, hypertension, diabetes, and influenza. Vitamin D is the most powerful anticancer agent ever discovered. Researchers say you should enjoy 20 to 30 minutes of sunshine before applying daily sunblock.

Recognize that it's not just our planet that revolves around the sun, but life itself. Through photosynthesis, plants convert sunlight into usable energy, kicking off the food chain and creating the foundation for the entire web of life. The sun is responsible for most of our energy, too. In *Chasing the Sun*, Richard Cohen writes:

> The Sun is the great self-renewing resource, the creator of coal, peat, oil, hydroelectricity, and natural gas. It raises moisture into the atmosphere, to return as the downpours that drive turbines; it powers the winds and the waves, and all their effects; it lavishes itself over the entire planet, delivering to the Earth's surface more energy in just forty-four minutes than we use in a year.

The Aztecs and Egyptians worshiped the sun, as did the Persians, Incas, and Tamils of southern India. Grand monuments to it still dot the globe, from the pillars of Stonehenge to the Great Pyramid at Giza to the temple ruins of Machu Picchu. This is not surprising, really. Consider how many ways the sun resembles the traditional image of a deity. It is a mysterious enigma, ever-present, powerful beyond measure, a giver of light, responsible for life on Earth, yet too terrible to gaze at directly. Sun worship stemmed from a fundamental truth: without our nearest star, life on Earth wouldn't exist.

Yet knowledge about the sun wasn't easily won. We had to wait for the advent of the telescope as well as the scientific method. Isaac Newton, in fact, spent so much time studying the sun that he had to shut himself in a darkened room to wait for the full return of his sight. It took three days. Dutch philosopher Spinoza ground the mirrors for his own telescope and died at 44, his lungs rotted from years of inhaling glass particles.

Early church authorities tried to strangle the science of astronomy in its cradle, insisting it undermined the Bible's geocentric view of the universe. Joshua commanded the *sun* to stand still, not the Earth, thundered Martin Luther. When Italian astronomer Giordano Bruno openly theorized that the sun was a star and the universe might contain other worlds, he was promptly put to the stake. Galileo, the father of observational astronomy, was forced to recant his heliocentric views and placed under lifelong house arrest. Scientists quickly got the message, privately declaring that it was better to be humble than hanged.

Progress and scientific understanding could not be stopped indefinitely, however. Today we know the sun influences crop yields, global temperatures, and ocean currents. Solar eruptions— caused by intense magnetic activity—affect the position and strength of the Gulf Stream, the frequency of auroras, the clarity of radio transmissions, the longevity of Earth satellites, the thickness of the atmosphere, and the condition of the ozone layer. The atoms that make up your body were forged in the heart of ancient suns. The iodine in your thyroid gland was fashioned from supernova material. The iron in your blood came from the cores of previous star generations. As Carl Sagan famously declared, we are *star stuff contemplating star stuff*.

The sun is the lamp of the world, an awe-inspiring, life-giving ball of fire, a constant source of comfort and wonder. Throughout history, it has dominated art, language, religion, and science. It is the great muse of artists, responsible for glorious sunsets, dazzling rainbows, and the ethereal Northern Lights.

Yet there is much about the sun we simply don't know. Scientists are still trying to understand what causes sunspots and solar winds, how its magnetic particles affect the Earth's climate, and how the sun's rays can be cost-effectively captured.

New spacecraft are even being designed to harness its power. Engineers are betting that someday—many years hence—it might be just the right fuel to carry us beyond our dying star's grasp and out of the solar system . . . in search of another sun.

■ THE MAN WHO INVENTED CHRISTMAS

My family, some friends, and I recently attended a performance of *A Christmas Carol* at the American Shakespeare Center in Staunton, Virginia.

It was a superb performance. The kids particularly enjoyed it and were surprised to learn that the author, Charles Dickens, is the man most responsible for the modern celebration of the season. This is a story that deserves to be more widely known.

Dickens is one of the greatest writers in the English language. He published 20 novels in his lifetime. None has ever been out of print. Yet in 1843, Dickens's popularity was at a low, his critical reputation diminished, his bank account overdrawn. Facing bankruptcy, he considered giving up writing fiction altogether.

In a feverish six-week period before Christmas, however, he wrote a small book that he hoped would keep his creditors at bay. But his publishers rejected it. So using his meager savings, Dickens put it out himself. It was an exercise in vanity publishing, and the author told friends it might be the end of his career as a novelist.

Yet the publication of *A Christmas Carol* caused an immediate sensation, selling out the first printing—several thousand copies—in four days. A second printing sold out before the New Year, and then a third. Widespread theatrical adaptations spread the story to still larger audiences. And it became one of the favorite books of the season globally over the next two centuries.

It wasn't just a commercial success. Even Dickens's chief rival and foremost critic, William Makepeace Thackeray, bowed his head before the power of the book: "The last two people I heard speak of it were women; neither knew the other, or the author, and both said, by way of criticism, 'God bless him!' What a feeling this is for a writer to be able to inspire, and what a reward to reap!"

Today, we all know the tale of tight-fisted Scrooge—"Bah! Humbug!"—and his dramatic change of heart after being visited by the ghosts of Christmas Past, Present, and Future. But *A Christmas Carol* didn't just restore Dickens's reputation and financial health. It also breathed new life into what was then a second-tier holiday that had fallen into disfavor. Employers even refused to give workers the day off.

As Les Standiford notes in *The Man Who Invented Christmas*, in early nineteenth-century England, the Christmas holiday "was a relatively minor affair that ranked far below Easter, causing little more stir than Memorial Day or St. George's Day today. In the eyes of the relatively enlightened Anglican Church, moreover, the entire enterprise smacked vaguely of paganism, and were there Puritans still around, acknowledging the holiday might have landed one in the stocks."

The date for Christmas is arbitrary, of course. There is no reference in the gospels to the birth of Jesus taking place on the 25th, or in any specific month. When Luke says, "For unto you is born this day in the city of David a Savior," there isn't the slightest indication when that was. And while the day was marked on Christian calendars, celebrations were muted. That changed when *A Christmas Carol* became an instant smash, stirring English men and women to both celebrate the holiday and remember the plight of the less fortunate. This was exactly the author's intent.

Dickens grew up in poverty, had only sporadic schooling, and was forced into child labor. (His father, a naval pay clerk who struggled to meet his obligations, was thrown into debtor's prison.) Yet despite these handicaps, Dickens educated himself, worked diligently, and rose to international prominence as a master writer and storyteller. He was a great believer in self-determination and, in particular, the transformative power of education. With learning, he said, a man "acquires for himself that property of soul which has in all times upheld struggling men of every degree."

Yet in the London of Dickens's day, only one child in three attended school. Some worked in shops, others in factories. Still others resorted to theft or prostitution to live. Dickens was determined to expose their plight and lead a crusade for public education. *A Christmas Carol* is a bald-faced parable, something few novelists attempt and even fewer successfully execute.

Dickens said his novels were for the edification of his audience. His goal was not just to entertain but to enlighten. And *A Christmas Carol* was designed to deliver "a sledge-hammer blow" on behalf of the poor and less fortunate. It worked. Scrooge—a character as well known as any in fiction—is now synonymous with "miser." Yet through his remarkable transformation, the author reminds us that it is never too late to change, to free ourselves from selfish preoccupations.

Dickens's biographer, Peter Ackroyd, and other commentators have credited the novelist with single-handedly creating the modern Christmas holiday. Not the contemporary orgy of shopping, spending, and ostentatious display, however. Recall that in *A Christmas Carol* there are no Christmas trees, gaudy decorations, or—apart from "the big, prize turkey" at the end—any presents at all. The only gifts exchanged are love, friendship, and goodwill.

In one small book, Dickens changed the culture, inspired his contemporaries, and helped restore a holiday they were eager to revive. More than a century and a half later, *A Christmas Carol* is still a tonic for our spirits and an annual reminder of the benefits of friendship, charity, and celebration.

Do You Know Where You Are?

In Robert Ludlum's novel *The Bourne Identity*—later made into a successful movie trilogy starring Matt Damon—the lead character, Jason Bourne, is a man with a debilitating amnesia. He can't make sense of his life because he doesn't know who he is or where he's from. Without a past, he has no identity.

Many of us are in a similar predicament. The difference is that we aren't doing anything about it. Let me explain . . .

Of course, you remember the key events and people from your past. You know where and when you were born and who your parents and grandparents were. And, while you may not know much about them, you realize that you had eight great grandparents, sixteen great-great grandparents, and countless other ancestors going back thousands of years.

But how about before that? How did your most distant ancestors arrive on the scene? And how about the scene itself? How old are the mountains, the seas, and the planet? When and how did the Earth start spinning on its axis and circling the sun?

Human beings have wrestled with these questions and others like them since time immemorial. We watched the tides and wondered what caused them. We puzzled over the twinkling lights in the sky at night. We trembled when volcanoes erupted or hurricanes blew. Ancient cultures tried to understand the natural world and our place in it, inventing stories and myths to explain it all.

But we didn't have the scientific method or the right tools, so we couldn't *know*.

Now we do know. Yet most of us haven't familiarized ourselves with the basic facts. There is a video clip from the show *Who Wants to Be a Millionaire* where a contestant is asked, "What orbits the Earth? A. The sun, B. The moon, C. Mars, or D. Venus."

The question is a lay-up. Yet the contestant agonizes over it. Finally, he decides to poll the audience, and 56 percent answer "the sun." It's tempting to believe that this was a fluke. Yet surveys regularly show that only 28 percent of American adults have the most basic scientific literacy. (Readers overseas shouldn't gloat. The Japanese and Europeans score even worse.)

The natural history of our planet—from its birth out of cosmic rubble to the beautiful land, sea, and sky we enjoy today—is an epic story. Yet, like Jason Bourne, most of us are entirely ignorant of our past.

Geology reveals that in its 4.6-billion-year history, the Earth has been everything from molten rock to a "frozen snowball" with surface ice up to a mile thick. Over the eons, astonishing changes took place. Water arrived with the bombardment of the planet by icy comets and meteors. Mountains rose up like waves. Rivers changed course. Species—at least 99.9 percent of them—arose and then died out. The continents broke apart and skated around the globe, and still move today.

Pulitzer Prize–winner John McPhee once said the dramatic geological history of the Earth can be summed up in a single sentence: The summit of Mt. Everest is marine limestone. How we came to know these things is a fascinating story. And understanding the mechanics doesn't diminish the beauty and majesty of the natural world—or its mystery. After all, there is still plenty we don't know.

Watching the moon rise in the evening sky, for example, it's tempting to believe it has always been there. Yet the evidence shows that four billion years ago the early Earth was struck by a protoplanet, blasting part of the mantle and crust into space. Over thousands of years, the debris gradually coalesced into the moon. (As a boy, I was taught there were 29 other moons in the solar system. But, thanks to the march of technology and a steady improvement in telescopes, we now know that a more accurate number is "at least 178." And that's *after* giving Pluto and its three moons the boot.)

Educators often argue that scientific literacy is necessary so that we can understand the scientific enterprise, argue public policy, and compete in a global economy. But there is a more fundamental reason. Like Jason Bourne, we need to know who and where we are and how we got here.

In its education guide, the National Academy of Sciences says, "Scientific literacy means that a person can ask, find, or determine answers to questions derived from curiosity about everyday experiences. It means that a person has the ability to describe and explain natural phenomena." Few of us have the time to wade through science textbooks, however, or spend our weekends roaming natural history museums. So let me suggest a few shortcuts: *Origins* by Neil deGrasse Tyson and Donald Goldsmith, *Life* by Richard Fortey, and *A Short History of Nearly Everything* by Bill Bryson are three superbly written books easily accessible to the layman. Another great starting point is a fine documentary from the National Geographic channel called *Earth: Making of a Planet*. (It's available uncut and in high definition on YouTube. I'll bet you can't watch it just once.)

Most of this stuff is not relevant to our work-a-day lives, of course. So why bother to know it? Because you can't know where you are if you don't know where you've been.

This knowledge should be an essential part of any liberal arts education. If you met an American who was ignorant of Christopher Columbus or Jamestown or the Revolution of 1776, you'd find it inexplicable. Is it any less absurd to know nothing about the history of the Earth, the only home we've ever known?

THE MIND-BOGGLING UNIVERSE, PART II

My last essay on the natural history of the Earth produced a flurry of letters from readers. Most respondents said they enjoyed taking a moment to consider the grandeur of the stars, moons, planets, and galaxies. But it can be just as fascinating to move in the opposite direction: the realm of the infinitesimally small.

One of the most profound and fundamental questions we can ask is "what is everything made of?" The answer is the elements. The periodic table, which arranges the building blocks of matter to reflect common properties, is one of the pinnacles of scientific achievement, the single most important unifying principle in chemistry. Science writer Theodore Gray calls it "the universal catalog of everything you can drop on your foot."

The elements are the primal stuff of creation. They cannot be separated into simpler substances. (This property of indivisibility is what makes an element *elemental*.) Elements, like gold or silver, may exist in their pure state or marry up to form compounds, as hydrogen and oxygen do to create water and sodium and chloride do to form salt.

We are made of elements, too, of course. And it is a humbling dish. It takes just four ingredients—carbon, nitrogen, oxygen, and hydrogen—to make up most of the molecules in your body. Cosmologists tell us the atoms in these molecules were forged in the fiery hearts of distant stars and blasted into space in a supernova explosion. It is a heady reminder of our connection with everything else. (As one wag put it, a physicist is just the atom's way of thinking about atoms.)

Human beings are part of the fabric of the universe. Every atom down here was once out there. And from this atomic architecture rises the structure of our large-scale world. In other words, not only are we in the universe, the universe is in us. It's hard to imagine a deeper feeling than that.

It seems wildly counterintuitive, but everything, both organic and inorganic—wood, metal, moss, and skin—is made of the same stuff. We stand on the elements, we eat the elements, we *are* the elements. We really can, as William Blake put it, "see a World in a grain of sand."

Contemplating our atomic structure in *A Short History of Nearly Everything*, Bill Bryson writes, "These tiny particles uncomplainingly engage in all the billions of deft, cooperative efforts necessary to keep you intact and let you experience the supremely agreeable but generally underappreciated state known as existence." He adds that if you were to pick yourself apart with tweezers, one atom at a time, you would produce a mound of fine atomic dust, none of which had ever been alive but all of which had once been you. (You may want to read that last sentence again and share these thoughts with a close friend over a good bottle of wine.)

We now know that atoms are made up of moving parts. The nucleus consists of protons and neutrons and is surrounded by a swarm of lighter electrons. Yet atoms are more than 99 percent empty space. (And that means everything else is, too.) If the nucleus of an atom were the size of a golf ball, the outermost electrons would be *two miles* away. Like galaxies, atoms are essentially cathedrals of cavernous space. Yet they form all the richness of our world.

In one of his famous lectures, the Nobel Prize–winning physicist and science popularizer Richard Feynmann said, "If, in some cataclysm, all of scientific knowledge were to be destroyed, and only one sentence passed on to the next generations of creatures, what statement would contain the most information in the fewest words? I think it is this: That all things are made of atoms—little particles that move around in perpetual motion, attracting each other when they are a little distance apart, but repelling each other upon being squeezed into each other."

The chair you're sitting on, for instance, appears solid, but is actually a constantly vibrating illusion. The reason you can't put your fist through it—at least, not without a good deal of anguish— is that the electromagnetic fields set up by atoms in the chair repel similar fields in your hand. As Einstein famously showed in his theory of special relativity, matter *is* energy.

Just about everything about the atomic world challenges our preconceptions. And our investigation into the subatomic realm reveals even deeper and more surprising mysteries. Unfortunately, few artists have yet embraced these ideas. And since our poets don't write about them and our musicians don't sing about them, we are generally reduced to hearing not a song or a poem but a lecture.

This is not always the case, however. In *The Periodic Kingdom*, chemist and author P. W. Atkins writes:

> The real world is a jumble of awesome complexity and immeasurable charm. Even the inanimate, inorganic world of rocks and stone, rivers and ocean, air and wind is a boundless wonder. Add to that the ingredient of life, and the wonder is multiplied almost beyond imagination. Yet all this wonder springs from about 100 components that are strung together, mixed, compacted, and linked, as letters are linked to form a literature. It was a great achievement of the early chemists to discover this reduction of the world to its components, the chemical elements. Such reduction does not destroy its charm but adds understanding to sensation, and this understanding deepens our delight.

We are still at the dawn of a scientific age. Yet the more we learn, the better we understand ourselves and our world.

It begins with the periodic kingdom. It tells us that no matter what you look at, if you look at it closely enough, you are looking at the whole universe.

The Best That Has Been Thought and Said

I've noticed something lately, an increasing acceptance of the view that—in today's wired society—it's no longer necessary to know or remember key facts.

According to this school of thought (to use the term loosely), it makes no sense to clutter your mind with names and dates, geography and science, tenets of philosophy, or turning points in history. After all, if you really need to know something, Google and Wikipedia are just a click away.

Surely there are a few of us left who don't consider our smartphones and tablets appendages. But even if you're connected 24/7, are you really going to hold up your hand during a conversation and say, "Bill of Rights. Hmm. That sounds important. Hold on. Let me just check something here"?

Shared meanings are essential for effective communication. In particular, reading comprehension requires more than just recognizing the words on the page. It requires broad specific knowledge. It isn't possible—and shouldn't be necessary—for a writer to explain who Leonardo da Vinci was, or when the Crusades happened, or what occurred at Yorktown. The reader should know.

Yet many today embrace the opposite view—and the picture is not a flattering one. For instance, Jay Leno does a standard set

piece where he quizzes passersby on the streets of L.A. In one epi-
sode, he asks a young man where the pope lives.

"England," he replies.

"Where in England?" Leno follows, keeping a straight face.

"Ummm, Paris."

He asks another pedestrian, "What's another name for the War
Between the States?" But the man protests. "Is this the kind of
stuff we're supposed to know off the top of our heads?"

The smart responses wind up on the cutting room floor, of
course. Correct answers aren't comedy. But Leno has tapped into
something very real. In a recent survey, 52 percent of high school
graduates chose Germany, Japan, or Italy over the Soviet Union as
a U.S. ally in World War II. A third put the Civil War in the twentieth century. Two-thirds could not explain a photo of a theater
whose portal reads "COLORED ENTRANCE." Yet 64 percent
could identify the Kardashians.

Increasingly, our culture debases more than it uplifts. Passive
entertainment has turned many adults into perpetual adolescents.
"We are increasingly ignorant," lamented W.A. Panapacker, "but we
do not know enough to be properly ashamed."

It wasn't always this way. Throughout most of the twentieth
century, there was massive demand among the middle class for
intellectual betterment. Individual volumes of Will and Ariel
Durant's 10,000-page magnum opus *The Story of Civilization*
climbed the *New York Times* best-seller list. Countless households
purchased the *Encyclopedia Britannica* and *Great Books* collections.
In the 1980s, millions tuned in to watch economist Milton's
Friedman's 10-hour PBS series "Free to Choose."

At the risk of sounding like a scold, much of today's popular
entertainment is mind-numbingly dull and facile. Yet a 2011 survey
by the U.S. Department of Labor's Bureau of Labor Statistics found
that Americans spend an average of 2.7 hours a day watching TV and
an equal amount online. Offline reading amounts to only 20 minutes a day. Using leisure time to acquire knowledge or understanding
is increasingly viewed as anachronistic, if the idea is considered at all.

We are particularly ignorant of history and civics. If you don't
know what is protected by the First Amendment, you can't do much

"critical thinking" about rights in the United States. If you don't know which countries border Israel, it's hard to fathom the situation in the Middle East. Basic facts like these—what some call *core knowledge*—are an indispensable starting point for deeper insight and genuine literacy. Part of the problem is the way history is taught. In *The History Boys*, playwright Alan Bennett points out that history is not taught as an unfolding of events, a series of power struggles, or even a clash of ideas, but rather "just one f------- thing after another."

And in no particular order, I might add. British historian Niall Ferguson suggests that only a tiny fraction of the public knows the chronological march (given here) of these key events: the Renaissance, the Reformation, the Scientific Revolution, the Enlightenment, the French Revolution, the Industrial Revolution, and the First World War.

If we don't know the order in which these things occurred, we can't make the causal connections. Historical events are unintelligible if they lack narrative flow or are remembered in the wrong order. Without an accurate timeline in your head, you can't think about things properly.

Ferguson writes in *Civilization*:

> Although the past is over, for two reasons it is indispensable to our understanding of what we experience today and what lies ahead of us tomorrow and thereafter. First, the current world population makes up approximately seven percent of all the human beings who have ever lived. The dead outnumber the living, in other words, fourteen to one, and we ignore the accumulated experience of such a huge majority of mankind at our peril. Second, the past is really the only reliable source of knowledge about the fleeting present and to the multiple futures that lie before us, only one of which will actually happen.

History informs us about today. We use historical insights to see the present more clearly, to understand what is happening and why, to decide what actions we need to take *now*. As Harry Truman observed, "The only thing new in this world is the history you don't know."

We easily outstrip our ancestors in wealth, creature comforts, health, and life span. We exceed them in the breadth of our political freedom and the security that governments provide. But a culture that does not know or understand the past risks the kind of backwardness that led Edward Gibbon to call the Romans at the apex of their empire "a race of pygmies." It is only through persistent seeking—the thirst to understand—that we achieve and appreciate great things.

Education, properly understood, is the occupation not of childhood, but of a whole life. We should each be on a quest to discover what Matthew Arnold famously called "the best which has been thought and said."

Fortunately, we have a breadth and ease of access far greater than what was available to earlier generations. And the cost has never been lower. In fact, much of it is free. There is plenty of great content available at iTunes University and Khan Academy. Conversations and lectures by brilliant historians like David McCullough, Gordon Wood, and Stephen Ambrose are available on YouTube. Or, if you prefer the analog world, you can always resort to the most beautiful word in the English language: the library.

There are practical reasons for remedying our ignorance, too. Recent research into the relationship between health and education found that better-educated people live longer and healthier lives. They have fewer heart attacks and are less likely to become obese and develop diabetes. We also know there is a direct correlation between a well-educated population and a stable, free society.

Too often, education is seen as something purely financial, vocational, or utilitarian. Many have lost sight of the lifelong ideal of simply becoming educated. We are the beneficiaries of an enormous civic and cultural inheritance. Should we not make some effort to understand it?

As Liel Leibovitz of *Tablet* writes:

> If you're serious about reading—or, for that matter, about your education—see to it attentively. Revisit Homer and read your way through human history. Don't stop until you reach Kafka. Or, better yet, don't stop until you see the entire vista of culture spread before you and feel yourself every bit a part of it.

A Titan for Freedom and Prosperity

Someone once quipped that economists are people who are good with numbers but don't have the personality to be accountants. Milton Friedman (1912–2006) was a glaring exception, a brilliant and tireless advocate of individual liberty and free markets—and a true intellectual giant.

Many historians regard diminutive James Madison, the fourth U.S. president and Father of the Constitution, as the brainiest of the Founders, one with "an astonishing ratio of mind to mass." Friedman, at five foot three, was the modern-day economic equivalent.

A winner of the Nobel Prize in Economics, the Presidential Medal of Freedom, and the National Medal of Science, there simply was no greater voice for economic freedom in the second half of the twentieth century. His 1971 book, *A Monetary History of the United States*, analyzed the Great Depression and changed the way we think about money. His classic *Capitalism and Freedom* (1962) explained why free markets are not just economically but ethically superior to even well-intentioned government plans. And his popular 10-part PBS series *Free to Choose* demonstrated to millions the transformative power of capitalism.

Yet his influence, and an understanding of the beauty of the free enterprise system, is fading in some quarters today. According to the Pew Research Center, only 50 percent of Americans have a favorable view of capitalism. This might be expected after years of financial bubbles, a weak economy, and wide fluctuations in household wealth. But capitalism, best understood as the economic expression of liberty, has made our world better in countless ways.

Two hundred years ago, 85 percent of the world's population lived on the equivalent of less than a dollar a day. Today, less than 15 percent do. What is responsible for the enormous spike in material prosperity? Part of the credit goes to science and technology. But it took something more pedestrian to transform the world's standard of living: the profit motive. This is hardly a bad thing. As Adam Smith wrote in *The Wealth of Nations* in 1776, "It is not from the benevolence of the butcher the brewer or the baker that we expect our dinner, but from their regard for their own interest."

Government doesn't provide us with food, clothing, shelter, health care, or the Callaway Limited Edition Diablo Octane Tour Driver. Businesses do. And in the process of meeting our economic wants and needs, public and private companies offer employment to millions, develop job skills and careers, support local communities, contribute to charitable organizations, pay billions in taxes, and, of course, provide financial rewards for owners and shareholders.

Detractors argue that capitalism is all about selfishness, greed, and exploitation. Yet capitalism merely promises that you can have anything you want if you provide enough other people with what *they* want. Economic freedom is about voluntary exchange for mutual benefit. That's why you hear two thank-you's whenever someone makes a transaction. The buyer says thanks because he wants the merchandise more than the money. The seller says it because he wants the money more than the merchandise. Capitalism is not a zero-sum game where one side wins and the other side loses. It's a win-win.

Unlike government, business is about freedom and individual choice, not coercion. If you don't like a particular company or its policies, you don't have to work for them, sell to them, or buy from them.

Businesses focused solely on short-term profits don't last long. If you cut corners on quality, your customers will leave. If you bargain with suppliers too hard, they won't trade with you. If you undervalue your key employees, they will take their talents elsewhere. It is in the best interests of business owners to make sure all stakeholders—employees, suppliers, customers, and communities—are satisfied.

Now, here's a news flash: Businesses are run by fallible human beings. Sometimes they make mistakes, breach contracts, use poor judgment, harm individuals, or damage the environment. When they do, the transgressors should be punished. But that doesn't make capitalism *wrong* any more than democracy is wrong when a congressman is found with stacks of hundred-dollar bills in his refrigerator.

Some Americans are rightly incensed that Big Business uses political connections and an army of lobbyists to curry favors and receive preferential treatment from federal, state, and local governments. But this crony capitalism—or, as I prefer, *crapitalism*—is a perversion of the free market system and a strong argument for democratic reforms. Unfortunately, government is reluctant to reform itself when changes weaken entrenched power. (Witness, for example, the death of term limits, something polls show a clear majority of Americans favor.)

Additionally, government bailouts of companies that are "too big to fail" make a mockery of our profit-*and-loss* system. Only a naïf would argue that it makes sense to privatize profits and stick taxpayers with losses. This merely incentivizes investment banks and other companies to take outsized risks. Yet in the case of both bailouts and crony capitalism, it is *government interference* that tarnishes the capitalist system. Businesses may have the right to ask, but—as Friedman pointed out—Congress has the responsibility to say no.

The free-market system is the reason we live in a classless society. Most wealthy Americans achieved their affluence not by inheritance but by starting and managing profitable businesses. Of course, many of us lack the time, the investment capital, or the experience necessary to found and run a successful business, but we can still own a piece of one through the quintessential expression of capitalism: the stock market. With even a modest amount of money, an individual can accumulate a stake in many of the world's great businesses. And it's easy. A click of the mouse and a five-dollar commission and you're in. Another click, another five bucks, and you're out. (Compare *that* to your typical real estate closing.)

And owning a piece of a company is a whole lot simpler than running one. You don't have to take out loans, sign personal guarantees, hire or fire employees, grapple with an avalanche of federal mandates and regulations, pay lawyers and accountants, or even show up for work. How great is that?

Some Americans today obsess over the issue of fairness. But the stock market shines here, too. If I own shares of Microsoft, for example, my gain over the next year will be exactly the same as the nation's richest man, Bill Gates. Sure, he may own a few more shares than I do, but our percentage returns will be the same.

In short, over the past few hundred years, capitalism has vastly improved our quality of life and standard of living. Milton Friedman understood this. He evangelized about it, sharing his conviction that personal freedom is the supreme good in economic, political, and social relations. And he was never angry or mean-spirited about it. He always pressed the case for capitalism and freedom with impeccable scholarship, good cheer, impressive vigor, and unmatched clarity. As former Secretary of State George Shultz once joked, "Everybody loves to argue with Milton, particularly when he isn't there."

For some, the advantages of free markets are so evident that a champion seems unnecessary. But that wasn't the case when Friedman began making a name for himself in the 1950s. Intellectuals and academics were enthralled by the possibilities of central planning and government control. Experience—and Milton Friedman—taught them otherwise.

When he died in 2006, *The Economist* described Friedman as "the most influential economist of the second half of the 20th century . . . possibly of all of it." His wife, Rose, a fellow economist and cowriter, died three years later.

The Friedmans were perfect for each other and understood what truly matters. In their memoir, *Two Lucky People*, they summarized their lives not in terms of best sellers, honors and prizes, material success, public service, or even their Foundation for Educational Choice, but with these words: "Our life has surpassed our wildest expectations: two wonderful children, four grandchildren, rewarding professional careers, and a loving partnership. Who could ask for more?"

THE GREAT KEY TO SUCCESSFUL LIVING

At a neighbor's party, I bumped into a distracted woman wearing a frown.

"Hey, don't hog *all* the fun," I said with a nudge.

She shook her head and offered a slightly embarrassed smile. "It's just that when I come to social events like these, I cringe when people ask what I do and I have to admit I'm a stay-at-home mom."

"What's wrong with that?" I asked. "You don't like having the most important job in the world?"

She sensed that some folks—especially working women—looked down on her. She felt marginalized. I was tempted to remind her of Eleanor Roosevelt's line that no one can make you feel inferior without your consent. But I took a different tack and told her about a story I'd just read in the *Philadelphia Inquirer*.

A budget crunch at the Philadelphia School District caused the district to lay off 91 school police officers. You might reasonably wonder why a school police force is necessary in the first place. But in the 2010 school year, 690 teachers were assaulted. In the past five years, more than 4,000 were.

The newspaper reported that in Philadelphia's 268 schools, "on an average day 25 students, teachers, or other staff members are beaten, robbed, sexually assaulted, or victims of other violent crimes." And that doesn't include thousands more who are extorted, threatened, or bullied each year. Why is this happening? The short answer is poor parenting. (Some might call it no parenting at all.)

There are few threats to our future greater than family disintegration. Forty-one percent of all children today are born to unmarried women, and the number rises to more than 50 percent for women under 30.

Single-parent households in the inner city often lead to disorderly neighborhoods, schools that cannot teach, transgenerational poverty, and mass incarceration. There are nearly 2.3 million people in American prisons and jails today. Another 5 million are on probation or parole. Knowing this, how could anyone really look down on someone dedicating a significant portion of his or her adult life to parenting? After all, the family is the foundation of all great societies.

Yet a parent's job has never been tougher. Modern culture doesn't elevate kids. It doesn't celebrate education, virtue, hard work, or risk taking. It distracts and consumes them with celebrity and materialism. Popular music and television shows cater to the lowest common denominator. Mindless consumption is idealized and encouraged by the most sophisticated marketing techniques ever devised.

In my house, we fought a constant battle with our 14-year-old daughter, who begged to go with her friends to PG-13 movies where glamorous young stars play characters who are drunk, high, and hopping from bed to bed with nary a consequence. (When I was young and childless, this seemed like a trivial issue. Funny how having kids changes your perspective.)

These developments put the burden squarely on Mom and Dad. Sixty years ago, parents raised their kids to adopt the values of the culture. Today, a big priority is getting them to reject the values of the culture. How do you do it? Mostly the old-fashioned way— by instilling values and setting an example.

It takes more than just teaching kids to behave, however. They also have to dream. And it's up to parents to show them the best way to achieve those dreams. That usually requires something specific . . .

In 1972, Stanford psychologist Walter Mischel concocted an ingenious experiment involving young children and a bag of marshmallows. He put a marshmallow on the table and told each child that if he (or she) could wait 15 minutes to eat it, they would get a second one as a reward. Two-thirds of the kids flunked miserably. Some caved in at once; videotapes show others struggling to discipline themselves, some even banging their little heads on the table.

But the surprising results of the study came years later. Researchers followed up on the children to see how their lives progressed. Turns out the kids who exercised forbearance rather than eating the marshmallows at once had SAT scores 210 points higher. They were also more likely to finish college, enjoyed significantly higher incomes, were far less likely to go to jail, and suffered fewer drug and alcohol problems.

What does this mean? It means we should love our kids. We should teach them to treat others the way they would want to be treated. But if we really want them to succeed in life, we should also teach them the enormous benefits of *delayed gratification*.

Think about it. Education takes time and persistence. Professional attainments require concentrated effort. Saving and investing—instead of spending—take discipline. Successful parenting means sacrifice and commitment. The bottom line? Kids should expect to struggle and learn to put off rewards. Because, with few exceptions, success means giving up what you'd like to do for what you ought to do.

Today, we live in a society of haves and have-nots. But to a great extent, that's because we also live in a society of wills and will-nots. Self-discipline—even more than much-vaunted self-esteem—is the key. This is a message every child should hear—and parents who embrace it should hold their heads high.

Even at a cocktail party.

What You Can Learn from "The Gadfly of Athens"

One of my all-time favorite intellectual heroes is Socrates. Born in Athens in 469 B.C., he was one of the greatest thinkers of all time, a founder of Western philosophy who devoted his life to learning. Yet he insisted that he had nothing to teach. Instead, he spent his days wandering through the great, teeming agora—the massive, 37-acre marketplace at the heart of ancient Athens—asking questions and debating the *essence* of what it means to be human.

Like Jesus of Nazareth, Socrates never jotted down a word. Everything we know of his life and ideas comes from the works of his students, Plato and Xenophon, and the plays of his contemporary, Aristophanes.

They describe him as an intellectual giant and master of irony who made lasting contributions to ethics, epistemology, and logic. He did *not*, however, cut a particularly fine figure. The Ancient Greeks made a fetish of human beauty, but Socrates was described as the ugliest man in Athens with his spindly bowlegs, paunch, hairy neck and shoulders, bald bumpy head, snub nose, protruding lips, and bulging eyes.

We also know he had an extremely ill-tempered wife, Xanthippe, reputedly "the most troublesome woman of all time." When asked why he married such a shrew, Socrates good-naturedly replied that he wanted to prove that there was no one he could not mollify.

I'm skeptical on this point. Socrates did not become "The Gadfly of Athens" by soothing souls. Rather, he encouraged his listeners to challenge arguments from authority and question even deeply held beliefs—*especially* deeply held beliefs. In doing so, he frustrated and embarrassed many powerful people with his persistent line of questioning, known today as the Socratic method.

Socrates wanted those around him to think deeply, critically, about how they spent their days. The most fundamental measure of time is a human life span, he declared. It is essential that we adopt a life-affirming ethic and imbue our lives with meaning.

He insisted that much of what he was taught as a young man was insupportable or wholly wrong. He was hostile to "received wisdom" and encouraged his students to challenge parents, teachers, politicians, religious leaders, and so-called experts.

With his probing questions, he became a master at exposing pretense and erroneous belief. He purported not to instruct but to "un-teach" men, arguing that the greatest obstacle to discovery is not ignorance but the illusion of knowledge.

Socrates stood for unfettered, unflinching philosophical inquiry. He wants to prevent us from clinging to unreflective thought. "The highest form of human excellence," he maintained, "is to question oneself and others."

Alarmists claimed that he was destabilizing Athenian society. There was a backlash. Socrates was accused, tried, and ultimately condemned to death on trumped-up charges of "impiety" and "corrupting the youth of Athens."

This was particularly shameful since Socrates was completely devoted to Athens. He never left it except to fight for it—and was shaped by its democratic ideals and its zeal to be the most forward-looking city-state on earth. But Socrates chose to accept his death sentence—by drinking the poisonous hemlock—rather than escaping or seeking exile. He upheld his principles to the end . . . and became a martyr to the independent mind.

What are the ideals that Socrates died for? He believed that life should be devoted to learning. Education and awareness makes you virtuous, he said, and virtue is the surest road to happiness. He believed that very little is necessary to live the good life. He delighted in reducing his needs to an absolute minimum, insisting that poverty is a shortcut to self-control and that the richest man is he who is content with the least. Observing the shop displays in the agora one day, he exclaimed, "How many things I can do without!"

Many of his best-known utterances still speak to us today:

- Employ your time in improving yourself by other men's writings, so that you shall gain easily what others have labored hard for.
- Prefer knowledge to wealth, for the one is transitory, the other perpetual.
- Be kind, for everyone you meet is fighting a hard battle.
- Beware the barrenness of a busy life. Leisure is the most valuable of possessions.
- We cannot live better than in seeking to become better.
- The greatest way to live with honor in this world is to be what we pretend to be.
- Let him who would move the world first move himself.

Ancient Greek culture is widely recognized as the foundation of Western culture. Before the Greeks, intellectual inquiry was always tainted by cant or superstition. Socrates helped change that with his insistence on reason and observation.

In the West today, we think the way we do, in large part, because Socrates thought the way he did. In his unwavering commitment to truth, he set the standard for philosophy and science. His questions disturbed, provoked, exhilarated, and intimidated his listeners. He insisted it is not enough to have the courage of your convictions. You must also have the courage to have your convictions *challenged*.

He encouraged his students to practice and refine the art of questioning. When you do, you develop a better sense of who you are, why you are here, and what you can be. Contrary to popular belief, the more questions you have, the *firmer* the footing you are on.

Socrates exemplified the philosopher's endless quest, a path where the goal is not just the finding but the seeking. Gregory Vlastos, a Socrates scholar and professor of philosophy at Princeton, describes Socrates's method of inquiry as "among the greatest achievements of humanity." Why? Because he demonstrated that *how we should live* is every individual's primary business.

Socrates was among the first to ponder deeply about what makes humans happy and how such blessings can be acquired. He inspires us to use the power of our own minds to approach the truth. And he compels us to seek a deeper understanding of what constitutes the Good Life.

Socrates was a philosophical genius, the quintessential seeker and conveyor of wisdom. We know this because his goal was not to show us *what* to think but rather *how* to think. As he famously put it, "The unexamined life is not worth living."

The True Rulers of the Planet

As I write, it's summertime. That makes it easy to hate bugs right now.

It's not just the occasional bite or sting or weekend picnic invasion. Insects devour about a third of the world's food crops each year. They destroy wooden buildings, ruin stored grain, and accelerate the process of decay. Mosquitoes, which transmit diseases like West Nile virus, malaria, and dengue fever, kill almost 2 million people annually. (Even tsetse flies are responsible for 66,000 annual deaths.) And bees kill more people each year than all poisonous snakes combined.

Insects are our biggest competitors for food, fiber, and other natural resources. Economists estimate that insects consume or destroy 10 percent of gross national product in large, industrialized countries and up to 25 percent of gross national product in some developing nations.

Yet before you shoo, squash, or swat that little fellow in front of you, pause to recognize that insects are also our cherished allies. Indeed, we could not exist without them. They were here 400 million years before us and, in many ways, still rule the planet.

Insects dominate the temperate zones, making up a significant percentage of the earth's total biomass. There are around 200 million insects for every person alive today—approximately 9 billion per square mile of habitable land. Ants alone, of which there may be 10,000 trillion, weigh roughly as much as all 7 billion human beings.

We have formally classified about 1 million species of insects so far. And we're only just getting started. Entomologists estimate that the total number ranges between 4 million and 30 million.

And they are amazingly diverse. We have identified 290,000 species of beetles, for example, yet millions more remain unclassified. Not only are there more types of insects than any other kind of animal, there are more types of beetles than any other kind of insect. When the distinguished British biologist J.B.S. Haldane was asked by a group of theologians what one could conclude about the nature of the creator from a study of the creation, Haldane replied, "An inordinate fondness for beetles."

We spend billions of dollars a year on pesticides and extermination services. Yet insects also make us (and save us) billions. A 2006 study by Cornell University entomologist John Losey found that bugs add $57 billion a year to the U.S. economy. Dung beetles save ranchers some $380 million a year by decomposing waste and helping return nutrients to the soil, reducing the need for fertilizers. Since they prey on each other, bugs also provide more than $4.5 billion in agricultural pest control. (Hey, it's organic.) And, since insects offer themselves up daily as food for native wildlife (from rainbow trout to ring-necked pheasants to black bears), they also support a $50 billion recreation industry in our national parks and wilderness areas.

Insects help solve world hunger, too. In the United States, more than 4 million bee colonies produce over 90,000 tons of honey annually. Total global honey production is estimated at 884,000 tons a year.

Many people in non-Western countries dine on locusts, ants, termites, caterpillars, grasshoppers, and grubs. According to informed sources (braver than I), beetles taste like apples, wasps like pine nuts, and worms (not really insects) like fried bacon. Advocates point out that bugs are high in protein and other nutrients. For instance, a 100-gram portion of grasshopper meat contains 20.6 grams of protein, just seven grams less than an equivalent portion of beef. In addition, insect farming requires less water, less feed, and less land per calorie than traditional livestock farming. It also produces much lower greenhouse gas emissions.

Insects, too, are invaluable tools for scientific research, thanks to their rapid reproduction rate and the ease of keeping them in laboratories. The first association between pathogens and disease grew out of Louis Pasteur's studies of silkworm diseases.

Grasshoppers and cockroaches are used as test animals to study the effect of chemicals on nerves. The geneticist's fruit fly has contributed greatly to our knowledge of chromosome structure, mutation, and sex-linked inheritance.

And the ecological services that insects provide are incalculable. Ladybugs, mantids, and other predatory insects eat aphids and other insects harmful to plants. Termites, while unwelcome behind your walls, decompose the wood in forests and help bring nutrients back to the soil. Many species of flowering plants owe their very existence to insect pollinators. Honeybees, in particular, are responsible for 80 percent of the pollination in the United States, affecting some $20 billion in crops each year, including almonds, apples, cherries, blueberries, cucumbers, squash, and melons.

In *The Creation*, Pulitzer Prize–winner and Harvard biologist E. O. Wilson writes:

> People need insects to survive, but insects do not need us. If all humankind were to disappear tomorrow, it is unlikely that a single insect species would go extinct, except three forms of human body and head lice. . . . But if insects were to vanish, the terrestrial environment would soon collapse into chaos.

He points out that a majority of flowering plants, deprived of their pollinators, would cease to reproduce. Birds, reptiles, and mammals, denied the foliage, fruits, and insect prey on which they feed, would follow the plants into oblivion. The soil would remain largely unturned because insects, not earthworms as generally supposed, are the principal renewers of the soil. A decline in soil quality would herald the end of wind-pollinated grasses and eventually the trees. Before long, human populations would experience widespread starvation and disappear.

Their small stature may prevent insects from being recognized as masters of the planet. But their importance and durability are beyond dispute. Insects witnessed the rise and fall of the dinosaurs. They have survived at least four major cataclysms that resulted in planet-wide extinctions. They continue to thrive despite mankind's best efforts at eradication. And they will very likely survive us.

Ours is a symbiotic relationship, but a skewed one. We *need* the insects. They *don't* need us. That leads to an odd and humbling thought: Just who is really bugging whom?

Confessions of an Analog Man

Okay, I was wrong.

When I realized a few years ago that almost everyone I knew was tweeting, texting, snap-chatting, and posting perpetual status updates on Facebook, I thought there would be an eventual backlash, a counterrevolution.

There won't be, apparently. The era of 24/7 connectivity is here. It's the future. And it's forever. Call me an anachronism, but I can sum up this development in a single word.

Yuck.

Yes, modern technology saves time, lowers costs, increases efficiency, and improves productivity. I work online. And I use the Internet to book flights and hotel rooms, pay bills, schedule appointments, watch my stocks, and check the news. But the rest of the time I'm unplugged. Call me a digital outcast, but I'm a free and contented one.

I'm grateful I grew up in a predigital world, one where my boyhood wasn't stolen by gee-whiz computer games and 400 cable channels; where my college years weren't spent texting, tweeting, and Web surfing; and young adulthood wasn't a nonstop barrage of mobile messages, e-mail alerts, and Facebook posts.

There's a downside to all this electronic gadgetry in our lives. But I'm surprised how few are doing much (if anything) to free themselves. Many seem not just immersed but addicted.

Think *addicted* is too strong a word? Consider this list of characteristics from the literature of recovery. It is meant to identify problems with drugs, alcohol, gambling, and overeating. Yet look at the similarities:

The Addictive Experience

1. Creates predictable, reliable sensations.
2. Becomes the primary focus and absorbs attention.
3. Temporarily eradicates pain and other negative sensations.
4. Provides an artificial sense of self-worth, power, control, security, intimacy, or accomplishment.
5. Exacerbates the problems and feelings it seeks to remedy.
6. Worsens functioning, creates loss of relationships.

In a recent Stanford University study, 75 percent of respondents admitted sleeping with their iPhone next to them in bed. Ninety-four percent confessed to feeling fixated or obsessed with it. The average teenager with a cell phone reportedly sends 60 text messages a day, almost 22,000 a year. And that's just *the average*. Among my 15-year-old daughter, Hannah, and her friends, there is hardly an unspoken thought. Excuse me, *untexted* thought.

Readers of a certain age are also surprised that it's no longer considered rude in many circles to whip out a phone in the middle of a meal or discussion and begin answering e-mails or sending texts. Its tough to have a conversation with someone who's looking down and mindlessly nodding his head while he communicates electronically with someone else.

This newfound connectivity isn't just disruptive. It's annoying. Elizabeth Bernstein of the *Wall Street Journal* recently published an open letter to set some digital ground rules:

Dear Family and Friends,
  I love you and miss you and want to hear from you. But you've got to stop spamming me.

Please quit sending me long, unsolicited, multipart texts and Skype video requests during work hours. Facebook messages I won't see for weeks. And those phone calls where you hang up without leaving a message.

And please, I beg you, stop calling my cell, home and office phones, sending me texts and emailing all of my accounts—all within the space of two minutes. . . .

I suppose I'm approaching advanced geezerhood, but the idea that you're supposed to continually monitor your Twitter account, e-mail, Facebook, cell phone, and land line in order to keep in touch isn't enticing. There is also the loss of intimacy, not to mention common sense and good taste. Consider a recent letter to columnist Judith Martin:

Dear Miss Manners:

In the past year, two male friends whom I have known for many years proposed marriage to me. I turned them both down due to the fact that both asked me in a text message. When did asking for a woman's hand in marriage become so impersonal?

Some will say I'm overstating things, that pervasive electronic communication is essentially harmless. It's not.

We all know that using a smartphone while driving or crossing the street is risky. But there is also evidence that it impairs the ability of adults to supervise young children. In the past five years, as smartphone use has grown sharply, the decades-long decrease in childhood injuries—thanks to everything from baby gates on staircases to fences around backyard pools—has suddenly reversed. According to a new report from the Consumer Product Safety Commission, since 2007, children under five have seen a 17.8 percent increase in unintentional falls, a 10.5 percent increase in objects in the eye and throat and—most disturbing—a 105.3 percent increase in near-drowning incidents.

Many parents (and sitters) believe they are *multitasking*. The truth is they are merely distracted.

Facebook is another dissipation. Yes, when your family and friends are spread across the country or around the world, it's easier and cheaper to stay in touch this way. You can see the wedding pictures. Hear about the job promotion. Or watch the baby take her first steps. All good. But social networks are also about something very different. When a status update says "The perfect gift from the perfect husband" or "Got another royalty check for the book!" or "Ran my best time this morning despite all the champagne on the plane last night," that's not sharing. That's crowing.

Millions are using Facebook to carefully stage-manage an online image. Does anyone really need to see photos of your suite at the Four Seasons or interior shots of your new Mercedes? These folks are using Facebook to one-up their "friends," many of whom they barely know. This is little more than an adult version of the kind of exclusionary bragging and bullying that goes on in middle school. Who really has time to play this game or watch someone else play it? As comedian Andy Borowitz put it, "There is a fine line between social networking and wasting your f------ life."

In many ways, technology has changed the fabric of our lives. But tweets, texts, and e-mails aren't conversation. Nor are they togetherness.

We think we are more connected than ever. But real life can ramp down as technology ramps up. There simply is no substitute for face-to-face interaction. Real conversations are awash in facial expressions, tones of voice, body language, and other nonverbal cues. There's a big difference between pushing a "like button" and seeing people laugh or smile.

In many ways the Internet is a godsend, yes. But it can also be depersonalizing. Dehumanizing even. The irony in all this connectivity is greater disconnectedness, an epidemic of distractedness and alienation. Not much in everyday life is more dispiriting than being at home with a family member and seeing only the back of his or her head.

We've all seen the bumper sticker "Hang Up and Drive." Maybe it's time to take it further. How about "Log Off and Live"?

How to Be Miserable in One Easy Lesson

At a conference in Las Vegas recently, I had the opportunity to meet and chat with Dr. Joel Wade, a psychotherapist who has dedicated his career to discovering what it means to live well. As a life coach, his practice is about helping people create and embody an extraordinary life.

His lecture was "Mastering Happiness: Practical Skills and Ideas for Living Well." When Dr. Wade uses the word *happiness*, however, he isn't talking about more parties, laughter, or high times. He's referring to something larger: having a sense that you are flourishing, of feeling fully satisfied with your life.

This is something we all desire, consciously or unconsciously, and virtually anyone can move closer to this ideal. Living a more satisfying life, Wade insists, is a skill that can be developed. It is mostly about the attitudes you embody and the choices you make. Like any skill, however, it requires time, attention, and dedication.

To illustrate his point, Wade demonstrated how easy it is to feel miserable. All that's necessary are three simple steps:

1. *Be as self-absorbed as possible.* Make sure every situation at work or at home is primarily about your thoughts, your

feelings. Make sure the point of every action is to accrue some personal benefit. Always ask "what's in it for me?"

2. *See yourself as a victim.* Observe that life has conspired against you. View others as the source of your problems. Blame them for your frustrations and setbacks. Tell yourself that you are helpless in your particular set of circumstances.

3. *Spend a lot of time ruminating.* Go over past negative events again and again. Think about things that make you angry. Dwell on what makes you bitter. Remember how you were hurt in the past and who was responsible. Spend a lot of time reliving and reexperiencing these events in your mind.

Just reading this short list, you probably feel a little bummed out. People who make these steps a habit are well on their way to a life of dissatisfaction and misery. The good news is that doing the opposite is a tonic and will almost certainly add to your satisfaction with life. In other words:

- *Absorb yourself in your work, friends, family relationships, and out-side interests.* Instead of asking "what's in it for me?" try "how can I help?" Get absorbed in what you're doing. Remind yourself what you are trying to achieve. And if you don't have personal goals—dreams with deadlines—set some.

- *See yourself as in control of your destiny.* We all have problems and setbacks, but things only begin to turn around when you take ownership of your situation. Then you can begin to move forward.

- *Focus on what's right with your life.* This is a tall order in some cases. Many of us are dealing with unfortunate economic or personal circumstances. Still, you can't wallow in it. Accept that the past is past. Forgive any transgressors, not for their sake but for yours. Start imagining how things could improve. This is the predisposition to action.

Dr. Wade points out that the best way to achieve a higher sense of well-being and life satisfaction is to cultivate a sense of gratitude.

He suggests taking a moment each evening to recall three things that happened during the day to make you feel grateful. It could be a problem resolved, an unexpected call from a friend, an unusually starry sky, or just a particularly good meal. Psychologists report that it is impossible to feel grateful and unhappy at the same time.

These steps may sound simple—and they are. But that doesn't mean they can't make a profound difference in your quality of life. As the British essayist Erich Heller observed, "Be careful how you interpret the world; it *is* like that."

FOR MUSIC LOVERS ONLY

At a FreedomFest conference in Las Vegas a few years ago, I participated in a panel discussion called "What Our Popular Music Says About Us."

When you look at Billboard's Hot 100 List—and see the boy bands, rappers, bubble gummers, faux country artists, and assorted Simon Cowell creations—you might be tempted to answer "nothing good." But, in truth, there has never been a better time for music lovers, even those with the most exacting standards.

Before you ask me to sit down and take my medication, hear me out. . . .

It is the natural progress of things, especially when we reach *a certain age*, to carp about how much better popular music was *back in the day*. Yet today, it is entirely and objectively true. Think about it. The 1940s gave us Nat "King" Cole, Duke Ellington, Louis Armstrong, and Bing Crosby. If you grew up in the 1950s, you had Chuck Berry, Elvis Presley, Patsy Cline, and Johnny Cash. The 1960s saw the heyday of Roy Orbison, Frank Sinatra, Jimi Hendrix, Bob Dylan, and the Beatles. The 1970s offered us the Eagles, the Stones, Bruce Springsteen, Marvin Gaye, and Bob Marley. (And this is only the snowflake on the tip of the iceberg. During the 1960s and 1970s, studios like Motown, Stax/Volt, and Sun Records churned out sheer genius week after week.) Things began to taper off in the 1980s, but you may still have enjoyed artists like Peter Gabriel, the Police, Tom Petty, or U2. And while the decline continued into the 1990s, at least bands like REM, the Black Crowes, Nirvana, Pearl Jam, and Radiohead gave rockers something to celebrate. In the past decade, however, things really hit the skids. Top-selling artists include 50 Cent, Justin Timberlake, Miley Cyrus, Flo Rida, Justin Bieber, and Ne-Yo.

Ne-Yo?

I am a lifelong music lover and collector, but can any pop album of the past 20 years be mentioned in the same breath as *Sgt. Pepper* or *Exile on Main Street*? Indeed, *Rolling Stone* recently released an updated list of *The 500 Greatest Albums of All Time*, and 292 of them—59 percent—were released in the 1960s or 1970s. Only two were released in the past decade, and one of those—*Smile* by the Beach Boys—was recorded 46 years ago.

Or forget albums—how about the singles? Where is this generation's "Eleanor Rigby," "Bridge Over Troubled Water," "Heard It Through the Grapevine," or "Fire and Rain"? They don't exist. Instead, the airwaves bombard us with misogynistic rap, boy bands that are really merchandising opportunities, and country music that sounds like Def Leppard with fiddles.

So why did I begin by arguing that this the best era for music lovers *ever*? Because there have never been more talented musicians playing more kinds of music in more venues than today. As for recorded sound, you have cheaper and easier access to more music, in more genres, from more eras, in more formats, than ever before.

Most of today's best-selling music is forgettable or unlistenable. But so what? You don't need to choose your music from Billboard's Hot 100 any more than you need to choose your reading material from the *New York Times* Bestseller List. (And perhaps that's a good thing given that, as I write, the nation's top three fiction best sellers are various *Shades of Grey*.)

Just as it makes no sense to read Danielle Steele before Mark Twain or look at Mark Rothko before Paul Cezanne, who would listen to Britney or Snoop Dogg before Ray Charles or Ella Fitzgerald? Or, if we're going to discuss immortal works, Mozart or Beethoven?

Some will say I've moved beyond the realm of popular music. Not so. Classical composers were the rock stars of their day. And the music was nothing if not popular. In the mid-nineteenth century, for instance, women would fall on Franz Liszt at his performances, tearing his clothes and fighting over locks of his hair. It may not have been the Beatles at Shea stadium, but it was a start.

Jazz, too, was popular music in the first half of the twentieth century. No one outsold Louis Armstrong, Benny Goodman, or Artie Shaw at the height of their fame.

Today, the free market allows you to indulge your musical tastes no matter how rarified or obscure. Maybe you like bebop. And not just bebop but post-bop. And maybe not just post-bop but electric bebop blended with funk? If you don't think something like that exists or could possibly be done well, you haven't heard the music of alto saxophonist Steve Coleman and his band, Five Elements, although you'd need to keep your mind wide open. (Imagine Charlie Parker jamming with James Brown.)

Today, you can also easily connect with beautiful and exotic music from all over the world. In my view, every record collection should include some reggae, fado, conjunto, and perhaps even a few ragas.

You can own whatever music you prefer—and inexpensively—in the format of your choice, from vinyl to compact discs to MP3 files. And there has never been higher-quality playback equipment available at a lower cost. If you are a music lover who is even moderately affluent, why limit yourself to a boom box or iPod? You owe it to yourself to hear a demonstration of an audiophile-quality system. In fact, if you've already splurged on an expensive home theater system, you may already have one and not know it. Try turning off the tube and popping a CD into the DVD player. (Yes, it *will* play it.) You might be surprised.

In short, there has never been a wider selection of great music available. It has never been less expensive to own relative to disposable income. Nor has it ever been easier to access it, buy it, carry it, or share it. So skip the Top 40 and put something good on.

And remember the words of Frank Zappa: "Information is not knowledge; knowledge is not wisdom; wisdom is not truth; truth is not beauty; beauty is not love; love is not music; music is the best."

PART TWO

A WEALTH OF WISDOM

From the beginning, I've argued that you are heir to *an embarrassment of riches*. This is evident in the opportunities you have, the freedoms you enjoy, and our unprecedented standard of living. But we have inherited something else priceless as well: thousands of years of wisdom about what it means to be human.

Literacy rates have never been higher. Key knowledge has never been cheaper or more widely available. All the best thoughts and suggestions from the wisest men and women of all time about how best to live are sitting on the shelves of your local library or, easier still, just a click or two away on the Internet.

Goethe said that he who cannot draw on 3,000 years of learning is living hand to mouth. It could just as well be said that individuals who do tap deeply into this rich cultural legacy are wealthy indeed. Yet the paradox is that much of this wisdom is buried in a sea of lesser books or like lost treasure beneath an ocean of online ignorance and trivia.

That doesn't mean that with a little bit of diligence you can't tap into it. Yet many people, perhaps most, never take advantage of all this human experience. They aren't obtaining knowledge beyond what they *need to know* for work or to get by. As a result, their view of our amazing world is diminished and their lives greatly circumscribed.

According to polls, for instance, only half of Americans accept that the universe began with the big bang. Apparently, they either don't know or refuse to believe that the hundreds of billions of other galaxies are all rapidly receding from us, and by running the tape backwards we know that roughly 13.7 billion years ago everything was compressed into an infinitely dense point. They don't realize that NASA's Explorer 66 (COBE) satellite confirmed the existence of the cosmic microwave background radiation—the echo of that cataclysmic explosion—that big bang cosmology predicted.

Likewise, nearly half of Americans believe mankind was created in a single day nearly 10,000 years ago. Science tells us that all living things evolved from simpler organisms and are connected through lines of genealogical descent. This theory is as well confirmed as the theory that the Earth goes around the sun.

Accepting these scientific findings doesn't make you anti-religious. Indeed, these tenets are accepted by the Catholic church, Reform Judaism, and most mainstream Protestant denominations. Yet I still meet plenty of smart, relatively well-educated people who are appalled, insulted, or closed-minded about the scientific explanation of our origins.

That's unfortunate because science does a good job of telling us the difference between what we would like to be true and what is really true. It has given us computers and vaccines and probed the recesses of the atom and the hinterlands of outer space. It is responsible for everything from the Internet to the artificial heart to a map of the human genome. New theories are tested experimentally every day. Some of them advance our knowledge. Those found wanting are rejected.

Science isn't without its limitations, of course. It can tell us how to build an atomic bomb, for instance, but doesn't address the significant question of whether to use it. But there is no conflict with scientific explanations and universal spiritual values. I have never heard a physicist or biologist argue against compassion . . . or forgiveness . . . or gratitude . . . or charity.

Moreover, for thousands of years, our ancestors gazed up at the sky at night and wondered about the stars, the planets, and their own origins. What they wouldn't have given to know the answers. Is it not a shame that science has now provided us with so many of these answers and yet the majority of us remain unaware?

By the same token, many brilliant men and women who have lived, laughed, suffered, and endured have left us their stories and the lessons they learned. By unplugging from our busy lives for a few minutes a day, we can learn from them and—over the course of our lives—enjoy this bountiful cultural inheritance.

WHERE CAN WISDOM BE FOUND?

When these essays were originally published, I received a note from a reader who thanked me for "sharing my wisdom." I appreciated the sentiment, but leaving aside for a moment how much—or how little—wisdom I might actually possess, is it possible for someone to transfer it to someone else? After all, wisdom is more than knowledge, more than experience.

The *American Heritage Dictionary* defines wisdom as "the ability to discern or judge what is true, right, or lasting." The *Shorter Oxford English Dictionary* goes a step further, defining it as "the combination of experience and knowledge with the ability to apply them judiciously." I prefer the second definition since true wisdom is only demonstrated by behavior. (And certainly not by short essays.) Our actions, not our words, reveal us.

Every society values wisdom, of course. The ancient Greeks and Romans considered it a key virtue. Eastern sages, too. The Book of Job tells us that the price of wisdom is above rubies. And Proverbs reminds us "with all thy getting, get understanding."

America's Founding Fathers are considered among the wisest revolutionaries of all time. John Adams was a scholar and Enlightenment political theorist. Benjamin Franklin—aside from being a scientist, inventor, and polymath—wrote an autobiography that is a study in the perfection of character. Thomas Jefferson, the quintessential

Renaissance man, warned that if "we leave the people in ignorance," old customs will return and "kings, priests and nobles . . . will rise up among us." America's founders believed we have a moral obligation to pursue wisdom.

But how do you acquire it?

It starts with desire. As a young man, for instance, I hadn't seen much, done much, or experienced much. But I was a constant reader. The more I read, however, the more self-conscious I became about my ignorance. So I doubled down and started reading twice as much. This exercise—an obsession that persists to this day—did little to remedy the problem. The great paradox of learning is the more you know, the more acutely you perceive how much you don't know, can't know, and probably never will know. Clearly, wisdom requires more than reading and education.

It requires time and experience, a key reason so many young men and women are whip-smart but deeply unwise. Better than enrolling in the school of hard knocks is learning through the experience of others. If you've had a teenager, however, you'll find your pearls aren't accepted with eagerness and gratitude. Some things have to be learned the hard way.

Take trading stocks, for example. I don't care how many books you read, how many seminars you attend, or how long you paper-trade your portfolio. Until you've felt the fear, greed, hope, and occasional terror of someone with actual skin in the game, you can't be a truly wise investor. Wall Street is littered with the bones of millions who understood that the goal is to buy low and sell high but could never bring themselves *to actually do it.*

Of course, you can learn to invest wisely, but wisdom itself is about something more important. It's about *how to live well.*

Fortunately, we have a bountiful inheritance, a few millennia of wise men and women to instruct us. Yet most of us don't have time enough to acquaint ourselves with their works.

There is a shortcut, however, a distillation of the best that has been thought and said. As Benjamin Disraeli put it, "There are men whose phrases are oracles; who condense in a sentence the secrets of life, who blurt out an aphorism that forms a character, or illustrates an existence." In any decent book of quotations, you will find many. A few of my personal favorites include:

Death twitches in my ear. "Live," he says, "I am coming."
—Virgil

It is almost impossible to overestimate the unimportance of most things.
—John Logue

Truly, the greatest gift you have to give is that of your own self-transformation.
—Lao Tzu

We don't see the world as it is. We see it as we are.
—Anais Nin

A man is rich in proportion to the number of things which he can afford to let alone.
—Henry David Thoreau

In silence a man can most readily preserve his integrity.
—Meister Eckhart

Perfect does not mean perfect actions in a perfect world, but appropriate actions in an imperfect one.
—R. H. Blythe

Many eyes go through the meadow, but few see the flowers in it.
—Ralph Waldo Emerson

It is better to know some of the questions than all of the answers.
—James Thurber

Dream as if you'll live forever. Live as if you'll die today.
—James Dean

The great thing in this world is not so much where we are, but in what direction we are moving.

—Oliver Wendell Holmes

Real joy comes not from ease or riches or from the praise of men, but from doing something worthwhile.

—Sir Wilfred Grenfell

A man's most valuable trait is a judicious sense of what not to believe.

—Euripides

In three words I can sum up everything I've learned about life: It goes on.

—Robert Frost

Wise sayings, all. Yet, until they are embodied in attitudes and habits, they are merely words.

Wisdom is an elusive concept. It entails a combination of knowledge, experience, discretion, and maturity, a sense of what is best worth knowing and doing. But to fully define and comprehend it may require more wisdom than we have.

Perhaps the best we can hope for is to keep approaching wisdom without ever achieving it. This recognition—that true understanding remains elusive—may be the best indication that we're gaining on it.

DISCOVERING A NEW SENSE OF THE SACRED

On March 6, 2009, NASA launched the Kepler Space Telescope to discover planets outside our solar system. Named after Johannes Kepler, the famous mathematician who devised the laws of planetary motion, it will monitor 100,000 stars similar to our sun for four years, keeping a lookout for habitable, Earth-sized planets.

Already, Kepler has found 15 extrasolar planets (beyond the more than 600 already known to exist) and identified up to 1,235 other candidates. Fifty-four of these are the right size and orbit a "habitable zone"—the goldilocks region neither too close to a sun nor too distant—where liquid water might pool on the surface of a planet.

It's a fantastic start, especially since Kepler has telescoped only a small part of the galaxy. Scientists believe that if we can find a planet with Earth-like conditions, we may ultimately find signs of extraterrestrial life.

No one can know the odds at this stage, but Dr. Alan Boss of the Carnegie Institution of Science estimates there may be a hundred billion habitable planets in the Milky Way. Astrophysicist Duncan Forgan of Edinburgh University suggests there could be thousands of intelligent civilizations in our galaxy alone. And the Hubble Space Telescope has uncovered over 100 billion other galaxies. It's enough to boggle the mind.

Four hundred years ago, Galileo's observations through his telescope proved that the Earth moved. In his *Dialogue Concerning the Two Chief World Systems*, he claimed that the sun and the planets did not circle the Earth, as was commonly believed. Rather, the Earth and the planets revolve around the sun.

This finding did not sit well with the Church. Galileo's pronouncements contradicted official Christian doctrine, specifically Chronicles 16:30, Psalm 93:1, Psalm 96:10, Psalm 104:5, and Ecclesiastes 1:5.

Galileo was hauled before the Inquisition, forced to recant, and found "vehemently guilty of heresy." His offending *Dialogue* was banned, and he was sentenced to formal imprisonment (later commuted to house arrest, which he remained under for the rest of his life).

In a letter to Kepler, Galileo complained that many of those who opposed his doctrines refused to look through his telescope, "even though I have freely and deliberately offered them the opportunity a thousand times."

The same prejudice persists in certain quarters today. Some don't like what microscopes, particle accelerators, spectrometers, and space telescopes tell us about the universe we live in. They complain about the "arrogance" of science. But the scientific enterprise is not just about discovery. It is also about humility. We strive to understand because *we know that we don't know.*

Science promotes knowledge and critical thinking. Conclusions are based on observation, experimentation, and replication. Beliefs that aren't supported by testable evidence aren't necessarily untrue. They just aren't science.

A few weeks ago, my grade-schooler brought home a worksheet describing the scientific enterprise. A scientist, it said:

- Shows curiosity and pursues answers to questions about the world.
- Maintains a balance of open-mindedness and skepticism by entertaining new ideas and challenging information not supported by good evidence.

- Respects the importance of reproducible data and testable hypotheses.
- Tolerates complexity and ambiguity.
- Persists in the face of uncertainties.

What is there to oppose here? In science, a fact is something confirmed to such a degree that it would be unreasonable to withhold assent. Conclusions are never final. Findings are always subject to revision.

Albert Einstein said, "All our science, measured against reality, is primitive and childlike—and yet it is the most precious thing we have." Isaac Newton said, "I do not know what I may appear to the world, but to myself I seem to have been only like a boy playing on the seashore, and diverting myself in now and then finding a smoother pebble or a prettier shell than ordinary, while the great ocean of truth lay all undiscovered before me."

Conceding what you don't know, admitting when you're wrong—these are strengths, not weaknesses. Pope John Paul II understood this. During his reign, he made over 100 public apologies for the Catholic church. In 2000, he apologized for its persecution of Galileo. (Better four centuries late than never.)

Today's Kepler mission is part of the centuries-old quest to expand our horizons and discover new worlds. It has generated intense interest and popular excitement. And why not?

Space exploration gives us a sense of awe and wonder. It is also a reminder that we belong to a planet, a galaxy, a cosmos that inspires devotion as much as discovery.

■ THE CASH VALUE OF
THE AMERICAN MIND

Although the Great Recession is behind us and the stock market has rebounded to new all-time highs, tough times remain for many Americans. Unemployment is high. Bankruptcies and foreclosures are near record levels. Repo lots are overflowing. Worry and stress are on the rise in many households.

Some of these folks might want to visit psychologist William James, even though he's been dead for a hundred years. James (1842–1910) was an author, philosopher, scientist, Harvard professor, and giant in American intellectual history.

He trained as a medical doctor but never practiced medicine. He broke new ground as a physiologist and psychologist. He studied religion and psychic phenomena and wrote three classic books, including *The Varieties of Religious Experience*, the acknowledged inspiration for the founding of Alcoholics Anonymous, one of the world's most effective treatment programs.

Although his name is not widely recognized outside academia today, James made major contributions to psychology, philosophy, literature, teaching, and religious studies. He coined numerous words and phrases including *pluralism, timeline, stream of consciousness, live option,* and *moral equivalent of war.* Historian Jacques Barzun writes that James's book *Principles of Psychology* is "an American masterpiece which, quite like *Moby Dick*, ought to be read from beginning to end at least once by every person professing to be educated. It a masterpiece in the classic and total sense."

What do so many find inspiring about James? In part, it was his life itself, his legendary zest for living. James loved to travel, hike, and mountain-climb. He served as a naturalist and accompanied Louis Agassiz on his expedition to explore the upper reaches of the Amazon. He churned out articles, books, and hundreds of public lectures while carrying a full teaching load at Harvard. When he died from heart failure in his late 60s, his contemporaries said he had literally worn himself out.

Despite James's many accomplishments, his life was not without its setbacks. He suffered from ailments of the eyes, skin, stomach, and back. He was diagnosed with neurasthenia and depression. He contracted smallpox in Brazil. Three siblings, including novelist Henry James and diarist Alice James, were afflicted with invalidism. His beloved sister, Alice, died of breast cancer at 44.

However, James believed that we are meant to spend our lives being curious, active, and fully engaged. He was also one of the first to try to reconcile science and religion. In particular, he was interested in human spiritual experience, a realm that is difficult to capture by logic or observation, and impossible to nail down scientifically.

Yet he found a way. James is the father of the distinctly American philosophy known as Pragmatism, the doctrine that truth reveals itself in practice, regardless of its origins. Something is true if it doesn't contradict known facts and *it works*.

James thought a belief should be judged by its results. He was more interested in the fruits of an idea than its roots and advised people to look for a truth's "cash value," arguing that a belief is *true* if it allows you to live a fuller, richer life.

He was particularly interested in showing men and women how to convert misery and unhappiness into growth. As you can see from some of his remarks, the approach is nothing if not pragmatic:

- Lives based on having are less free than lives based either on doing or being.

- Acceptance of what has happened is the first step to overcoming the consequences of any misfortune.
- If you believe that feeling bad or worrying long enough will change a past or future event, then you are residing on another planet with a different reality system.
- Great emergencies and crises show us how much greater our vital resources are than we had supposed.
- Compared with what we ought to be, we are half awake.
- Action may not bring happiness but there is no happiness without action.
- Believe that life is worth living and your belief will help create the fact.
- Act as if what you do makes a difference. It does.
- Begin to be now what you will be hereafter.

James taught that we can change our lives by altering our attitudes of mind. He called pessimism "a disease" and said it could be cured by substitution. You can change, for example, "I have to exercise today" to "I get to exercise today." "I get to visit my grandmother" can be substituted for "I have to visit my grandmother." The shift is a subtle one, but powerful.

The essence of a belief is the establishment of a habit, a willingness to act. That begins with a change of mind. The best motivation is always an inspiriting attitude.

As a pioneering psychologist, James's primary interest was how the mind can bring about life-changing effects. Yes, we can grouse about circumstances. But it is not what fate does to us that matters. What matters is what we do with what fate hands us.

"All that the human heart wants," declared James, "is its chance."

THE KEY TO CIVILITY
. . . AND GREATNESS

On a recent trip to Mount Vernon, I had the pleasure of hearing historian Richard Norton Smith deliver the second of three planned talks on the life of George Washington.

Washington, of course, is best known as the leader of the Continental Army, the first president of the United States, and the man who presided over the convention that drafted the American Constitution, the document that not only limited his power but became a model and inspiration for free people everywhere. Many historians regard Washington as "The Indispensable Man," the crucial Founding Father and one of the two or three greatest presidents ever.

Yet while most of us are familiar with Washington's major achievements, few know much about the man himself. And the little we do know is usually folklore or myth. Young Washington never chopped down a cherry tree. He did tell the occasional lie. And his dentures were *not* made of wood. (They were actually made of hippopotamus ivory.)

But the important thing to know about Washington the man is that he impressed his contemporaries as much by his extraordinary character as with his accomplishments. Everything about his presence and demeanor commanded respect. Over six feet two inches tall, Washington held himself ramrod straight, was always impeccably dressed, and displayed the manners of a European court. On first meeting him in 1774, Abigail Adams wrote to her husband, John Adams:

> You had prepared me to entertain a favorable opinion of him, but I thought the half was not told me. Dignity with ease and complacency, the gentleman and the soldier look agreeably blended in him. Modesty marks every line and feature of his face.

Washington worked on developing his character from an early age. As a teenage boy, he admired and copied into a little notebook *110 Rules for Civil Behavior* that originated from a Jesuit textbook. He took the rules to heart, carrying the handwritten list with him from his military days at Valley Forge and Yorktown to his two terms as president.

Some of them are antiquated. It is unlikely, for example, that you need to be reminded to "Spit not into the fire" or "Kill no vermin, fleas, lice or ticks in the sight of others." But most of his rules describe a simple decency that is often lacking today. He wrote, for example:

- Every action done in company ought to be with some sign of respect to those that are present.
- Do not speak badly of those who are absent.
- When in superior company, speak not until you are asked a question.
- Sleep not when others speak, sit not when others stand, speak not when you should hold your peace, walk not on when others stop.
- Show not yourself glad at the misfortune of another.
- Do not overtly value your own accomplishments.
- When you speak, be concise.
- Submit your ideas with humility.
- If you are corrected, take it without argument. If you were wrongly judged, correct it later.
- Do not be hasty in believing disparaging reports about others.
- Associate yourself with men of good quality if you esteem your own reputation. It is better to be alone than in bad company.

- Do not reprehend others when it is not your place to do so.
- Do not be curious about the affairs of others.
- Labor to keep alive in your breast that little spark of celestial fire called conscience.

To Washington, it was not enough to be well born, well connected, or well educated. You had to be—above all—a person of character. He believed that the inner man is cultivated by perfecting the outer man. You show integrity in how you treat others, especially those with whom you profoundly disagree.

All this is not to suggest that Washington was without his faults. Like virtually all plantation owners of his day, he was a slaveholder. (Although Washington was the only Founding Father to free his slaves.) He made military blunders and many errors of judgment, including trusting Benedict Arnold right up until he ran off to the enemy. And he was famous throughout his life for a volcanic temper. After one cabinet meeting, Thomas Jefferson recorded that President Washington "got into one of those passions when he cannot command himself."

Yet Washington endeared himself to his contemporaries because he combined authority with modesty, skepticism, and doubt. He was honored, praised—even revered by his fellow countrymen—like no American since. Yet he never lost sight of his shared sense of humanity. In Robert Frost's words, Washington was "one of the few, in the whole history of the world, who was not carried away by power."

He was recognized for his generosity, too. Historian David McCullough notes, "Once, when a friend came to say he hadn't money enough to send his son to college, Washington agreed to help—providing a hundred pounds in all, a sizable sum then—and with the hope, as he wrote, that the boy's education would 'not only promote his own happiness, but the future welfare of others.'"

Washington contributed $20,000 in stock to the founding of what would become Washington and Lee University in Virginia. His gift was the largest donation ever made to any educational institution in the nation until then, and has since grown to a substantial part of the endowment.

But two acts, above all others, show the extraordinary nature of the man. The first was when Washington surrendered his sword to Congress after defeating the British army.

When George III heard that General Washington—having risked everything, suffered much, and defeated the most powerful army on earth—had relinquished his command, turned the nation over to his countrymen and gone back to Mount Vernon, he declared, "If that is true, he'll be the greatest man in the world."

The second act was when he voluntarily resigned the presidency after his second term, setting a national precedent for the peaceful, orderly transfer of power. As Daniel Webster wrote, "America has furnished to the world the character of Washington, and if our American institutions had done nothing else, that alone would have entitled them to the respect of mankind."

To Washington, only civility, conscience, and character can create the harmony, the unity essential to the survival of a republic. Turns out that the man most responsible for self-government showed the world that what's really important is how you govern yourself.

How to Defeat Death

Driving through the Blue Ridge Mountains not long ago, I listened again to Ben Sidran's haunting *Concert for García Lorca*, a superb, Grammy-nominated jazz CD now sadly out of print (but available on iTunes).

Who was García Lorca?

Federico García Lorca (1898–1936) was the most important Spanish poet and dramatist of the twentieth century, known the world over for the beauty, clarity, and lyricism of his poems. American poet W. S. Merwin, who translated much of his work, said it would be impossible to imagine modern poetry without him. Pablo Neruda said, "I have never seen grace and genius, a winged heart and a crystalline waterfall, come together in anyone else as they did in him."

Unfortunately, García Lorca was abducted and assassinated by an anti-communist death squad who opposed his political views and—bizarrely—believed he was secretly communicating with the Russians through a transmitter in his piano. He was just 38.

Aside from his poetry, García Lorca is best known for his essay on *duende*, which he defined as "that mysterious power that everyone feels but no philosopher can explain."

El duende is a style of living, one that acknowledges the ever-present shadow of death and accepts that beauty and horror, the transcendent and the repugnant, exist side by side. It is a poignant melancholy. The Spanish philosopher Miguel de Unamuno called it "the tragic sense of life."

In the performing arts, jazz, blues, and flamenco embody *duende*. So does the distinctive Portuguese folk music known as *fado*. Love songs have *duende* if they express joy while also embracing the potential for sorrow and pain. American popular artists with *duende* include Bob Dylan, Van Morrison, Neil Young, and Tom Waits.

Duende is not an intellectual concept, but a poet's conception of the unforgiving place where the soul confronts deep emotion and the capacity for suffering. And nothing causes greater suffering than death.

García Lorca sought the sharp experience of life that is only realized by a heightened awareness of our own mortality. He said the best art reminds us that we are all living "on the rim of the well."

His words had a profound impact on Sidran, a renowned jazz musician as well as a journalist, author, and scholar with a PhD in American studies from Sussex University. In his memoir, *A Life in the Music*, he writes:

My whole life had been a search for "higher understanding," only to discover that there is no understanding higher than simply *being*. . . . For me, if life was a lesson, that was the teaching. Everything else, all the internal chatter—I need something, I *need* something—was just my way of trying to stave off the inevitable, to fill up the silences, to think my way past the unthinkable. Trying to avoid the fragility of life, in the end, I discovered that fragility was all there is.

In his *Concert for García Lorca*, Sidran praises the poet's art and the spirit of *duende*. The music is not about despair, however, but how to triumph over it. In his lyrics, often spoken instead of sung, Sidran quotes García Lorca's contemporary, the Spanish Roman Catholic de Unamuno:

To act in such a way as to make our annihilation an injustice, in such a way as to make our brothers, our sons, and our brothers' sons (and their daughters), feel that we ought not to have died, this is the way we are impelled to stamp others with our seal, to perpetuate ourselves in them and in their children. . . . This is the way *death* is *defeated*."

THE SAGE WHO SPOKE TO EVERYMAN

At the Shanghai Restaurant in Charlottesville one night, the fortune in my cookie said, "Confucius say when everything is coming your way . . . you are in the wrong lane."

Like most one-line fortunes, it didn't evoke belly laughs. But it was a reminder that in the West today, we rarely hear the name Confucius unless it's part of a punch line..

Yet the man was one of the great figures in the history of human thought. Confucius was a philosopher, educator, social critic, and political scientist. He addressed core human issues—morality, behavior, business, politics, and spirituality—with such clarity and precision that his sayings have been preserved and studied over thousands of years.

However, information about his life (551–479 B.C.E.) is scanty at best. Confucius was born in the feudal state of Lu in what is now Shantung province. And while he never held high office, his teachings on morality and purpose have greatly influenced the course of world history.

The central concept of Confucius's philosophy is *ren*, meaning benevolence. (The word also means "gentleman" in the sense of someone who behaves with authentic respect and consideration for others.) It was Confucius's view that the cultivation of benevolence leads to self-mastery and, ultimately, right action.

Confucius taught his pupils ethics, rhetoric, literature, and the arts. He did not lecture but asked questions, quoted classics, and employed analogies and parables, letting his students find the answers or see the points he was guiding them toward. Most of what we know of Confucius's teachings is based on the *Analects*, a collection of his sayings compiled from what was remembered by his disciples. It is a basic source for a wide range of advice on human affairs, from governing nations to improving personal relationships.

Confucius emphasized nobility. And he insisted this is a matter of behavior, not of birth. We become noble, regardless of our station in life, when we live according to true values. He encouraged his followers to strive to become *sages*. Sagehood is the full flowering of the individual, a benevolent and human-hearted path. Everyday life is the focus. Making it the best it can be is the goal. You achieve this, Confucius said, by awakening your inner wisdom and tapping your potential. How? His vision is laid out in the *Analects*:

- *Good people strengthen themselves ceaselessly.* Confucius said a united society and just government could be achieved only through the cultivation of the exemplary individual, the sage. *"Don't worry that no one recognizes you,"* he said, *"seek to be worthy of recognition."*

- *Good people nurture character with fruitful action.* Confucius believed no one could become virtuous by shunning society. Virtue must always be expressed in action. You should be slow to speak, he said, but quick to act.

- *Good people understand matters of justice.* He warned that ambition often causes individuals to cut corners—and regret it. *"Better that one who knows what is right is one who is fond of what is right; and better that one who is fond of what is right is one who delights in what is right."*

- *Good people refine cultured qualities.* Confucius esteemed the arts and believed they transmit the highest and best feelings. Great art—poetry, paintings, music, literature—allows you to experience life deeply and with greater sensitivity. *"By poetry the mind is aroused; from music the finish is received. The odes stimulate the mind. They induce self-contemplation. They teach the art of sensibility. They help to restrain resentment."*

■ *Good people educate themselves.* Learning is a highly valued activity for the Confucian sage, the path to enlightenment. Yet the great philosopher emphatically said that he would not do people's thinking for them. Through learning, we engage in the quest for wisdom, always pointing toward improvement in action. Knowledge leads to the development of the higher self. With wisdom, however, comes the recognition that there is always more to learn. Learning is infinite, ceaseless throughout life. Confucius argued that education is never an end in itself but a means of shaping and perfecting the individual for the betterment of society.

■ *Good people are parsimonious with power.* Today's Chinese leaders would do well to revisit this Confucian tenet and grant their citizens greater freedom. *"Exemplary people concern themselves with virtue,"* said Confucius. *"Small people concern themselves with territory."*

■ *Good people practice introspection.* Confucius told his followers to be hard on themselves and less so on others. Rare is the individual, he said, who can see his own faults and hold himself accountable. More than 500 years later, we hear this thought echoed in the New Testament: Why do you see the speck that is in your brother's eye, but do not notice the log that is in your own?" (Matthew 7:3)

■ *Good people inspire others.* Confucius believed our behavior should be a model for others. *"Cultivated people have nine thoughts,"* he said. *"When they look, they think of how to see clearly. When they listen, they think of how to hear keenly. In regard to their appearance, they think of what is appropriate. In their demeanor, they think of how to be respectful. In their speech, they think of how to be truthful. In their work, they think of how to be serious. When in doubt, they think of how to pose questions. When angry, they think of trouble. When they see gain to be had, they think of justice."*

■ *Good people enjoy life but are moderate in eating and drinking.* Confucius believed mealtime should be a ritual. You should invite special people to join you in a deliciously cooked meal. The food does not have to be expensive, but should be carefully and delicately prepared. Set the table formally: use your good dishes, silverware, and napkins. Place everything in its correct position. Play soft music. Light candles. Eat until you are satisfied, he counseled, but not until you are full.

Confucius inspires us to express our better natures. He reminds us that we define ourselves by what we do in our daily routines and relationships. These interactions provide us with the opportunity to show love, honor, and respect toward family, friends, teachers, and colleagues. Every action you take is a step toward this, in a positive direction, or a step away from this, in a negative direction.

Confucius's teachings transcended his life and became an inseparable part of China's great civilization and culture. Ralph Waldo Emerson called him "the George Washington of the world of thought." European philosopher Karl Jaspers grouped him among the world's greatest philosophers: Socrates, Buddha, and Jesus. Voltaire said, "To realize the theories of Confucius would bring about the happiest and most valuable period of human history."

Perhaps this is because Confucius speaks to everyman. He reminds us that virtue is not necessarily associated with grandiose works. There are plenty of opportunities to develop it in the course of ordinary interactions and undertakings.

And while Confucius confessed that he often fell short of his own ideals, he insisted that the highest purpose a man can have is to become the best version of himself.

THE GREATEST BEST SELLER OF ALL TIME

The word *spiritual* may be the most nebulous word in the English language. When I started the *Spiritual Wealth* project more than five years ago, I used the term not to argue for or against any religious point of view, but rather as a general term to distinguish the content from our usual investment discussions about material wealth.

However, many readers conflate the term with a particular religious perspective and so I was regularly asked, "Where is the Bible in your Spiritual Wealth?" I'm no biblical scholar, but as the book is a cornerstone of Western culture—and we recently passed the 400th anniversary of the King James Version—let's pause to consider it.

In England in 1604, an extraordinary group of 47 clergymen, scholars, and translators—authorized by King James and divided into six committees—began laboring intensively at Westminster, Oxford, and Cambridge. Seven years later, they completed the King James Version, a famously eloquent and beautiful translation that rendered the Old and New Testaments into crystalline English prose.

It quickly became an object of inspiration, instruction, and devotion. (Indeed, "Do unto others as you would have them do unto you" may be the best encapsulation of ethical wisdom ever articulated.) The King James Version had a monumental effect on our language. Hundreds of everyday phrases originated there, including "labor of love," "skin of your teeth," "bird in the hand," "drop in the bucket," "the powers that be," "bite the dust," "eat, drink and be merry," "salt of the earth," "see eye to eye," "out of the mouths of babes," "go the extra mile," "in the twinkling of an eye," "ends of the earth," "old as the hills," "the handwriting was on the wall," "the straight and narrow," "give up the ghost," and, perhaps most famously, "turn the other cheek."

In his plays, Shakespeare alludes to the King James Bible more than 1,300 times. Coleridge, Donne, and Milton, among other immortal poets, mined its riches. And its grand language and powerful message inspired American novelists from Herman Melville and William Faulkner to Saul Bellow and Toni Morrison.

The Bible has had an incalculable influence on art, literature, philosophy, government, philanthropy, and education. Teddy Roosevelt, hardly a Bible-thumper, said: "A thorough knowledge of the Bible is worth more than a college education." No one in the English-speaking world can be considered literate without a basic knowledge of it.

It is the most influential book ever written. It is not just the best-selling book of all time. It is the best-selling book every year. Worldwide, more than 80 million copies are sold annually.

The Bible, of course, has been used for purposes both good and ill throughout its history. It has engendered faith, hope, and charity as well as violence, sectarianism, and intolerance. It provided the theological underpinnings for American independence, the abolition of slavery, women's suffrage, and the U.S. civil rights movement as well as the divine right of kings, the Crusades, the Inquisition, and the Salem witch trials.

Its poetry and prose remain unsurpassed. Yet, aside from the letters of Paul and a few other exceptions, much of the Good Book's authorship remains unknown. In *Who Wrote the Bible?* Richard Elliott Friedman notes:

People have been reading the Bible for nearly two thousand years. They have taken it literally, figuratively and symbolically. They have regarded it as divinely dictated, revealed, or inspired, or as a human creation. They have acquired more copies of it than of any other book. It is quoted (and misquoted) more than the others as well. It is called a great work of literature, the first work of history. It is at the heart of Christianity and Judaism. Ministers, priests, and rabbis preach it. Scholars spend their lives studying and teaching it in seminaries. People read it, study it, admire it, disdain it, write about it, argue about it, and love it. People have lived by it and died by it. And we do not know who wrote it.

Archaeologists and historians are still putting the pieces together, but much of the Bible's history is shrouded in the mists of time. Traditional attributions vary. There are no original copies of the books that make up the Old and New Testaments, or even copies of copies of copies of the originals. Most of the teachings were passed down orally at first, transferred to scrolls many generations later, and today bear the inky fingerprints of hundreds of anonymous writers, editors, and translators down through the ages.

Yet the Bible is an amazingly enduring document, the most controversial and influential text of all time and a major force in the development of Western culture. Yet there is still widespread ignorance about its contents.

Pollster George Gallup has dubbed America "a nation of biblical illiterates." Only half of Americans can name even one of the four Gospels. The majority cannot name the first book of the Bible. Less than a third know who delivered the Sermon on the Mount. Fewer still can identify the Trinity or explain what Easter commemorates. The most widely quoted Bible verse in the United States—"The Lord helps those who help themselves"—is not in the Bible.

In 1924, in an argument about whether Spanish should be used in Lone Star schools, Texas Governor Miriam "Ma" Ferguson proudly declared, "If the King's English was good enough for Jesus Christ, it's good enough for the children of Texas." It's hard to know whether to laugh or cry.

The Bible has always meant different things to different people. To Jews and Christians, it is the Book of Books, the Word of God.

They have invested these writings with their greatest fears, highest aspirations, and most extravagant hopes. Others are less devout but consider the Book an unsurpassed guide to wisdom and moral action. Still others consider it the supreme work of literature, one that infuses the entire Western canon.

Many of today's most heated arguments revolve around what in the Bible is to be taken literally. One of the most haunting scenes in Genesis, for example, is when Jacob wrestles all night with a mysterious stranger and discovers in the morning that he had been struggling with God. Perhaps the best question the modern reader can ask is not where did it happen, when did it happen, or how can we be sure it happened, but rather "what does this passage mean?"

In *In the Beginning: A New Interpretation of Genesis*, religion scholar Karen Armstrong writes:

> In almost all cultures, scripture has been one of the tools that men and women have used to apprehend a dimension that transcends their normal lives. People have turned to their holy books not to acquire information but to have an experience. They have encountered a reality there that goes beyond their normal existence but endows it with ultimate significance. . . . It has helped human beings to cultivate a sense of the eternal and the absolute in the midst of the transient world in which they find themselves."

This sentiment is perhaps best expressed in an injunction from Saint Paul's Epistle to the Philippians: *Finally, brethren, whatsoever things are true, whatsoever things are honest, whatsoever things are just, whatsoever things are pure, whatsoever things are lovely, whatsoever things are of good report; if there be any virtue, and if there be any praise, think on these things.*

The Pursuit of Moral Perfection

A number of exceptional men and women were present at the founding of the United States. Few, however, matched the sheer genius of Benjamin Franklin.

He was a printer, postman, scientist, musician, inventor, author, activist, statesman, and diplomat. He was a major figure in the history of physics, discovering new theories of electricity. He invented bifocals, the lightning rod, the Franklin stove, a carriage odometer, and the glass harmonica. He formed the first public lending library in America and the first fire department in Pennsylvania.

Franklin was a member of the *Committee of Five* that drafted the Declaration of Independence. He was our first ambassador to France, an early abolitionist, and a key player at the Constitutional Convention of 1787. Yet in the second half of his life, after building the most successful publishing empire in colonial America, he scaled back his career in order to devote most his time to learning, civic activities, and philanthropy.

When his mother expressed puzzlement, he explained to her, "I would rather have it said, 'He lived usefully,' than 'He died rich.'"

Franklin decided to pursue what he called "moral perfection," a phrase that, in today's world, may sound proud, pompous, sanctimonious, . . . or unrealistic. But Franklin believed the new republic could survive only if the people were virtuous. It was widely reported that at the close of the Constitutional Convention a woman in the crowd called out, "Mr. Franklin! What kind of a government have you given us?"

He replied, "A Republic, Madam, if you can keep it."

He was right. Witness how fledgling democracies often falter in nations where there is widespread hatred, mistrust, or ethnic rivalries.

Franklin rejected the religious austerity of his Puritan parents, however. Instead, he spent much of his life seeking the "codes of behavior" that would help him and his fellow Americans live meaningful lives in an uncertain world. Over the years, he devised a plan to cultivate his character by 13 virtues. His autobiography— a literary classic and paean to the value of education, thrift, honesty, and hard work—lists these virtues as:

1. Temperance. Eat not to dullness; drink not to elevation.
2. Silence. Speak not but what may benefit others or yourself; avoid trifling conversation.
3. Order. Let all your things have their places; let each part of your business have its time.
4. Resolution. Resolve to perform what you ought; perform without fail what you resolve.
5. Frugality. Make no expense but to do good to others or yourself; i.e., waste nothing.
6. Industry. Lose no time; be always employed in something useful; cut off all unnecessary actions.
7. Sincerity. Use no hurtful deceit; think innocently and justly, and, if you speak, speak accordingly.
8. Justice. Wrong none by doing injuries, or omitting the benefits that are your duty.
9. Moderation. Avoid extremes; forbear resenting injuries so much as you think they deserve.
10. Cleanliness. Tolerate no uncleanliness in body, clothes, or habitation.
11. Tranquility. Be not disturbed at trifles, or at accidents common or unavoidable.
12. Chastity. Rarely use venery but for health or offspring, never to dullness, weakness, or the injury of your own or another's peace or reputation.
13. Humility. Imitate Jesus and Socrates.

Franklin insisted it was too ambitious to tackle all 13 virtues at once. Instead, he advocated working on one and only one virtue each week, then repeating the process after 13 weeks.

A realist, Franklin conceded that he often fell short of these standards. Yet he said just the attempt made him a better man and contributed greatly to his success and happiness. In his autobiography, Franklin wrote, "I hope, therefore, that some of my descendants may follow the example and reap the benefit."

How Apple Got Its Zen

I was surprised and saddened when I received news that Apple cofounder and CEO Steve Jobs had died. He was a hero of mine, a man who had a tremendous influence on technology, business, engineering, design . . . even culture.

Over a period of three decades, Jobs launched a series of products that transformed entire industries:

- The Apple II, the first personal computer that was not just for hobbyists.
- The Macintosh, which jump-started the home computer industry and popularized the graphical user interface.
- *Toy Story* and other Pixar blockbusters, which revolutionized digital animation.
- The iPod, which changed the way we store and listen to music.
- The iTunes store, which transformed the way we buy music and rescued the recording industry from rampant online piracy.
- The iPhone, which turned mobile phones into digital assistants with music, video, photography, and Web browsing.
- The iPad, which launched the tablet computing revolution.
- The iCloud, which demoted the computer from its central role in managing content and allowed devices to sync seamlessly.

◼ And let's not forget those ever-crowded Apple stores (where business is so good no one bothers picking up the phone when it rings), which reinvented the role of a store in defining a brand.

It's a shock to consider that a single individual oversaw the creation of so many different technologies that affect the way we work and play. Yet Jobs, a visionary thinker with a mercurial temperament, was not an easy man to understand. Biographer Walter Isaacson says he was powerfully shaped as a young man by his efforts to practice the tenets of Zen. He even traveled to Asia to immerse himself in the philosophy and, over time, it became deeply ingrained in his personality.

Zen is not well understood in the West. (I personally don't use the term unless I'm describing my favorite linguine with white clam sauce.) But after reading Isaacson's biography and the influence it had on Jobs, I looked into it a little further.

"Zen is not religion," writes Laurence Boldt. "If it means anything, it means to be awake, to bring full presence and consciousness to who you are and what you do. It comes from a deep yearning to express your inborn talents, gifts and abilities . . . Zen allows you to experience your everyday life as art by bringing to it the qualities of the artist—inspiration and absorption, creativity and resourcefulness, play and delight."

You could see this in Jobs's whole approach of stark, minimalist aesthetics and intense focus. While the competition churned out dull beige boxes each year, Apple introduced everything from translucent cubes to candy-colored space pods. Perhaps part of this was Jobs's cultivation of an awareness that applies to everyday life and work.

"Zen is the integration of the spiritual and the mundane," said Japanese essayist D. T. Suzuki, "an attempt to see the sacred in the ordinary. It is what turns one's humdrum life, a life of monotonous, uninspiring commonplaces, into one of art, full of genuine inner creativity."

This was apparent in Jobs's legendary fetish for design excellence. In an early version of the Macintosh, for instance, he upbraided a designer because the circuit board was "ugly."

"But it's inside the machine," replied the engineer. "No one will see it. No one will know."

"We'll know," said Jobs. The circuit board was changed.

Jobs believed that beauty is the by-product of doing things well or, in his words, "insanely great." That could result only from aspiring to perfection.

"Think different" was, for a time, Apple's short, ungrammatical slogan. That, too, is the essence of the Zen mindset. The idea is to attain wisdom and enlightenment through an immediate, unreflected grasp of reality.

Most of us imagine our grasp of reality is just fine, thank you. But that may be part of the problem. As Christian apologist C. S. Lewis wrote:

> Five senses; an incurably abstract intellect; a haphazardly selective memory; a set of preconceptions and assumptions so numerous that I can never examine more than a minority of them—never become even conscious of them all. How much of total reality can such an apparatus let through?

Zen encourages you to let go of preconceptions, to stop cherishing opinions. See the world as it is, not as you imagine it. Only then can you begin to change it . . . or at least change yourself. Zen also encourages you to take responsibility for your life, to be here now, to live in the moment, and to develop a more skillful perspective. You can see your life as a struggle to survive, to get and to spend . . . or as an opportunity for a creative performance. Steve Jobs chose the latter path and became an icon of imagination and invention.

He was just one in a long line of prominent Westerners who embraced the Zen point of view. Other diverse sages include Meister Eckhardt, Carl Jung, Erich Fromm, Robert Pirsig, Ludwig

Wittgenstein, Bertrand Russell, Aldous Huxley, John Cage, and Yogi Berra. (Perhaps especially Yogi Berra, who is famous for his Zen-like utterances, such as this one about a once-trendy restaurant: "Nobody goes there anymore. It's too crowded.")

The Zen approach says don't waste your time in idle complaint; roll up your sleeves and get to work. Steve Jobs did that—and the world beat a path to his door. He and his team created objects of excellence and beauty that made Apple an international symbol of quality and innovation and—with its more than $400 billion market cap—the most successful company in the world.

The Secret of "Big-Ass Salads"

If modern science offered a pill that could reduce your risk of heart disease, stroke, diabetes, serious infections, dementia, and even cancer by up to 88 percent with no negative side effects, would you take it? Most would answer with an unequivocal "Yes!" After all, who wouldn't want to live a longer, happier, healthier life?

There is no such pill, of course. But there is a simple, straightforward, and, quite frankly, *better* way to achieve this kind of "super immunity," one that allows you to achieve optimal health and maximum disease resistance. It does, however, have a serious side effect I'll describe in a moment.

What is this revolutionary life protector and extender I'm referring to? It's the food you eat. Or, more to the point, the food you should be eating but probably *aren't*, at least not in sufficient quantities.

I say this because most Americans are unaware of the ground-shaking advances made in nutritional science over the past decade. There is now overwhelming evidence that eating the right combination of foods can double or even triple the protective power of your immune system. This dramatically lowers your risk of getting everything from a cold or flu to serious infections to cancer.

Please be skeptical. I know I was until, while visiting a friend in Austin, I had the opportunity to meet (and cross tennis racquets with) Dr. Joel Fuhrman, a nutritional scientist, researcher, and board-certified family physician who specializes in preventing and reversing disease through nutrition.

What he shared with me—and spells out in detail in his book *Eat to Live*—astonished me. Dr. Fuhrman has shown thousands of patients and millions of viewers of his top-rated PBS specials how to protect and repair their health with great-tasting, natural foods.

In recent years, the evidence has grown that the *noncaloric* micronutrients in our food are vital to providing disease resistance and greater longevity. Scientists have discovered hundreds of phytochemicals (micronutrients found in plants) that evolved to help plants ward off disease in the wild. Our species survived by consuming large quantities of these plants. In short, *our* chemistry is dependent on *their* chemistry. Yet only in the past decade have scientists begun to understand how plants protect our health by boosting our immune systems.

Dr. Fuhrman calls phytochemicals "the most important discovery in human nutrition in the last fifty years." Among other benefits, they protect your cells from damage by toxins, help repair DNA, control the production of free radicals, and deactivate cancer-causing agents.

The lifetime probability of being diagnosed with an invasive cancer is now 44 percent for men and 37 percent for women. One in four deaths in the United States is due to this deadly disease. This rise in cancer incidence correlates almost perfectly with a major change in how we eat. Today's Western diet is so rich in processed foods and animal products—and so low in essential fruits and vegetables—that almost all Americans are deficient in plant-derived phytochemicals. Studies show that most of us consume less than 10 percent of our calories from the most nutritious foods: fruits, vegetables, beans, and seeds. Yet even this figure is misleading, because if you remove white potato products, including French fries and chips, vegetables make up less than 5 percent of our diet.

Instead of eating healthy, natural foods, Americans are gorging on processed foods: white bread, bagels, donuts, cold cereals, chips, pretzels, pasta, cookies, breakfast bars, and soft drinks. Yet a diet deficient in phytochemicals weakens your immune system.

The ramifications are sobering. The number of people suffering from immune system disorders, allergies, and autoimmune diseases is rising. Diabetes has become epidemic. And, according to the latest issue of the journal *Neurology*, not only are strokes now the fourth-leading cause of death in the United States, but patients are getting steadily younger. Men and women between 20 and 54 now make up 19 percent of all stroke patients.

But there is good news, too. Here are just a few of the latest discoveries in nutritional science:

- A review of more than 200 epidemiological studies shows that eating raw green vegetables has a consistent and powerful association with reduction of stomach, pancreas, colon, and breast cancer. (As one researcher put it, "You want to know the real secret to superior health? Big-ass salads.")
- People with the highest amounts of lycopene (an antioxidant found in tomatoes) in their blood are 55 percent less likely to have a stroke than those with the lowest levels.
- Twenty-eight servings of vegetables per week decreases prostate cancer risk by 33 percent. But just three servings of *cruciferous* vegetables each week—kale, collards, broccoli, or Brussels sprouts—decreases prostate cancer risk by 41 percent.
- One or more servings of cabbage per week reduces the occurrence of pancreatic cancer by 38 percent.
- White, cremini, portobello, oyster, maitake, and reishi mushrooms prevent DNA damage, slow cancer cell growth, and prevent tumors from acquiring a blood supply. Frequent consumption of mushrooms can decrease the incidence of breast cancer up to 70 percent.
- People who eat one-half cup of chopped onions a day may not have the freshest breath, but studies show they have a 56

percent reduction in colon cancer, a 73 percent reduction in ovarian cancer, a 71 percent reduction in prostate cancer, a 50 percent reduction in stomach cancer, and an 88 percent reduction in esophageal cancer.

- Multiple controlled studies show that pomegranates inhibit breast cancer, prostate cancer, colon cancer, and leukemia. They also naturally lower your blood pressure, help reverse atherosclerosis, and improve heart health.
- Many types of berries are rich in antioxidants, but elderberries also enhance the body's defense against viral infections, particularly influenza.
- Nuts and seeds are high in fat and calories but have been demonstrated in hundreds of medical studies to dramatically extend life and protect against disease. Indeed, as nut consumption increases, death from all causes decreases while overall life span increases.

It is hardly breaking news that fruits and vegetables are good for you. But Dr. Fuhrman is not just recommending that you eat more of them. To achieve maximum immunity and longevity, he suggests you make fruits, vegetables, beans, seeds, and nuts your primary diet. Other foods—such as whole grains, eggs, meat, fish, and fat-free dairy—should make up less than 20 percent of your total intake.

Dr. Fuhrman isn't just reviewing the latest studies. His experience treating over 10,000 patients using micronutrient-rich diets has demonstrated extraordinary therapeutic results over a wide range of serious health conditions. In *Super Immunity*, he writes:

Adding mushrooms to the diet lowers cancer rates, adding onions to the diet lowers cancer rates, adding greens to the diet lowers cancer rates, and adding blackberries to the diet lowers cancer rates. However, my argument and recommendations are for people not just to eat these foods, but to eat these foods in *significant amounts and simultaneously*.

He says each day you should have:

- At least one large salad.
- At least a half-cup serving of beans (perhaps in a soup, salad, or other dish).
- At least three fresh fruits, especially berries, pomegranate seeds, cherries, plums, and oranges.
- At least one ounce of raw nuts and seeds.
- At least one large (double-size) serving of green vegetables, raw or steamed.

Supplements, he argues, are no substitute for a healthy diet. In fact, to the extent that they give takers the confidence to eat in a less wholesome way, they are hurtful, not helpful.

I should also mention drinking. There are health benefits to drinking moderate amounts of alcohol, described as two drinks or glasses of wine a day for men or one for women. But as alcohol consumption goes up, so does the risk of cancer of the mouth, esophagus, pharynx, larynx, liver, and breast, according to the National Cancer Institute. And in a review of studies on alcohol and cancer risk published in the journal *Nutrition and Cancer* in 2011, Italian researchers found that heavy drinking—four or more drinks a day—was associated with a fivefold increase in the risk of head and neck cancers, as well as the higher risk of breast, colorectal, and pancreatic cancer.

I've been following Dr. Fuhrman's regimen myself (with a few tumbles off the wagon) and, while it was a bit of a struggle at first, I feel better today than ever. I'm also more than 20 pounds lighter. This is the "serious" side effect I referred to earlier. Folks on a nutritarian diet have a tendency to reach their ideal weight quickly.

It is widely recognized that most dieters fail to keep off the pounds they lose. However, there are good reasons to believe Dr. Furhman's approach is not only more effective but longer lasting. After all, this is not about being able to fit into your old pants or a new dress for a high-school reunion. It's about becoming as healthy and disease resistant as possible. When your food choices are driven not by vanity but rather a sincere desire to reach optimal health, the changes you make are more likely to become permanent, a new lifestyle instead of a passing fad.

Dr. Furhman's approach is not alternative medicine. It's progressive science. It's about harnessing the power of superior nutrition to preserve, protect, and extend your life. Isn't it good to know that one of the best things you can do to improve your health is under your own control and that it doesn't require you to visit another doctor, undergo more diagnostic tests, receive another shot, or take a new handful of pills? Science is telling us that a natural diet rich in micronutrients and antioxidants is a key to repairing immune system defects that may lead to disease.

This information isn't just new. It's transformational.

■ TAKE A VACATION INSIDE YOUR HEAD

On a recent tour of Italy, I got to know Dr. Satinder Swaroop, a cardiologist based in Fountain Valley, California. Among the many topics we discussed during our 10 days together was Transcendental Meditation (TM).

Dr. Swaroop is a lifelong meditator. And he has found that his patients who practice it enjoy better heart health. They are less anxious and sleep better. Their chest pains are less frequent. They are more able to stay on a diet and lower their cholesterol levels. They are calmer, too. He suggested I give it a try.

I don't have heart issues. I'm not an anxious person. If anything, I lean toward the overly mellow. Dr. Swaroop just smiled. "You should try it and see what happens." I told him I'd look into it.

A few weeks after I returned home, Dr. Swaroop sent me an e-mail. Had I visited TM.org as he suggested?

Uh, no.

"You should," he said again. "Just check out a couple of the videos."

And so I did. That's when I stumbled across a five-minute short by filmmaker David Lynch and became intrigued. I began reading up on TM and listening to people who practiced it. A week later, I signed up with an instructor.

I would have scoffed at this idea a few years ago. To the extent that I thought about meditation at all, I considered it a somewhat hippie, vaguely self-indulgent practice tied to Eastern religions or mystical "woo-woo" of one kind or another. Meditation seemed too . . . well . . . flaky.

But that view changed as I became more familiar with the scientific literature. There is an astonishing amount of research on meditation's physical and psychological benefits, including hundreds of peer-reviewed articles. Researchers have found that TM spreads a wave of calmness across the brain, organizing the prefrontal region in a way that improves focus and decision making. Studies also suggest it enhances physical health and increases longevity. How? By helping people deal effectively with stress.

In today's hectic and competitive world, stress wears us down and burns us out. It fuels countless disorders, including anxiety, insomnia, and depression. It also promotes cardiovascular disease, obesity, diabetes, and digestive disorders. Exercising and eating better can help counteract this. But meditation helps practitioners develop mental resilience, as well. The benefits are well documented.

In *Transcendence*, psychologist and educator Dr. Norman Rosenthal writes:

> A great deal of clinical research has been done on TM. For example, we now know that when people practice TM, their blood pressure drops. They show higher blood levels of a soothing hormone called *prolactin*, as well as more coherent brain wave patterns, which are associated with good mental functioning. New evidence suggests that TM may improve longevity and lower medical costs by reducing hospital stays and doctors' visits. Even people who are not in physical or psychological distress can be helped. TM has been shown to help "normal" people reach their full potential and live in greater harmony with one another.

Transcendental Meditation is not a religion. No one who practices it is asked to accept any belief system. The technique goes back thousands of years and was brought to the United States by Maharishi Mahesh Yogi, an Indian teacher who extracted the meditative technique from its Vedic origins and distilled it to its essence. Today, it is practiced by people of all religions and no religion.

How does it work?

TM is not learned from a book or video. It is taught by a certified instructor and experienced meditator. The process has seven steps: two lectures, a personal interview with the teacher, then four teaching sessions on four consecutive days.

Essentially, the student is taught to sit with hands folded in an upright chair in a quiet place. After a brief ceremony of gratitude, the instructor gives him his own mantra (a two-syllable wordless sound) to think about as he sits in quiet relaxation for 20 minutes twice a day. Ideally, this would be first thing in the morning and again in the late afternoon or early evening. (The mantra is simply a mental "vehicle" to let the mind settle down.)

In the beginning, I wondered how I would possibly find time to fit two 20-minute sessions into days already crammed with research, writing, traveling, speaking, exercising, socializing, and raising a family. But since no new skill can be learned without practice, I made time.

I haven't been at it long enough to report anything world changing. But I will pass along a few observations. First, there's something inherently pleasurable about taking a break from your daily routine to sit in quiet contemplation. Meditation helps you sort through all the mental flotsam and jetsam your mind throws up. The typical meditative session results in greater relaxation, inner peacefulness, and, occasionally, an enjoyable shift in consciousness.

Insights like these are hardly new, of course. Meditation has been practiced in both the East and West for thousands of years. In the second century A.D., the Roman emperor Marcus Aurelius wrote in his *Meditations*:

> Men seek retreats for themselves in country places, on beaches and mountains, and you yourself are wont to long for such retreats, but that is altogether unenlightened when it is possible at any hour you please to find a retreat within yourself. For nowhere can a man withdraw to a more untroubled quietude than in his own soul.

Psychologists report that in a typical day we process up to 70,000 thoughts and this continues even as we sleep. (Basically, the brain never shuts up.) Meditation is a pleasant and peaceful retreat, a tool for stilling the mind.

Thoughts or worries will arise during TM, too, of course. But meditators are counseled not to argue with or analyze them, but rather just to acknowledge them and let them go. Experienced meditators often report a blissful state of acceptance, serenity, and a feeling of being at one with the world.

TM is easy to learn and practice. It is less expensive than analysis, safer than prescriptions, and available for a lifetime without special equipment or facilities. Researchers have discovered that sitting with your eyes closed and repeating a mantra twice a day can cut your risk of serious disease by half. And it has no adverse side effects. If TM were a drug, it would be a multibillion-dollar blockbuster.

As Rosenthal writes:

> I have found most long-time meditators to be physically relaxed in their posture, alert in their expressions, and open-minded in their attitudes. It is not surprising that this demeanor and approach to life, played out day after day over years, would make a huge difference to health, longevity, and just plain enjoyment of life.

The good news is you don't have to follow a guru, visit an ashram, recite Sanskrit, or get into the lotus position on a hardwood floor. All you need is a comfortable chair, a quiet space, and 20 minutes.

And I invite you to be skeptical. I've learned it works for skeptics, too.

THE BIGGEST QUESTION OF THEM ALL

Scientists struggle with three really big questions today: How did life begin? How did human consciousness arise? And—oldest and toughest of them all—why is there something rather than nothing?

As a boy, I sometimes lay in bed at night puzzling over these. There can't be an end of space, I thought, because there must be something beyond *that*. And there couldn't be a beginning of time because there had to be a time before *then*. The more I mulled over eternity and infinity, the more it bothered me. It wasn't just that I didn't know the answer. I couldn't imagine that there *was* an answer.

So I pestered my Sunday school instructor. He told me only God could understand, and that He existed outside of space and time.

That seemed like a cop-out to me. "What does it mean to exist outside of space and time?" I asked. "What did He do, just boot-strap Himself into existence?"

He shrugged his shoulders and smiled. He seemed perfectly satisfied not knowing. Even at such a young age, this struck me as premature intellectual closure.

Today, physicists, astronomers, and cosmologists are working to understand the origins of the universe. Journalist and essayist Jim Holt came out with an excellent book on the subject in 2012 entitled *Why Does the World Exist?*

In various publications and for years, I had clipped out book reviews and articles by Holt on science, mathematics, and philosophy. I enjoyed his stuff but was certain I'd never met him. Then one day, out of the blue, my Dad said, "You know, Jane Holt's son Jim writes for the *New York Times.*"

"Jim Holt *the writer* is the same Jim Holt who lived up the street and went to high school with me, the one whose younger brother Bob used to school me in tennis and ping-pong?"

Yep.

I'd noticed in the bio at the end of his pieces that Holt . . . er Jim . . . was writing a book on "the puzzle of existence." Billed as "an existential detective story," *Why Does the World Exist?* tackles the question from several angles—scientific, mathematical, philosophical, and theological—and offers possible explanations in the manner of trial balloons.

Jim calls this the super-ultimate *why* question. And he's in good company. The British astrophysicist Sir Bernard Lovell said pondering it "could tear the individual's mind asunder." (Psychiatric patients have been known to obsess over it.) Intellectual historian Arthur Lovejoy said the attempt to answer it "constitutes one of the most grandiose enterprises of the human intellect." Philosopher Arthur Schopenhauer insisted the question was so large that no thinking person could ignore it. "The lower a man is in intellectual respect," he said, "the less puzzling and mysterious existence itself is to him."

In the past 100 years, we've learned a lot about the origins of the universe. In 1929, for instance, astronomer Edwin Hubble observed at the Mount Wilson Observatory in California that galaxies everywhere are rapidly receding from us. Run the tape backward and it becomes clear that roughly 13.7 billion years ago the universe was compressed into an almost infinitely dense point. (Yet another explanation that defies imagination.) What happened before that isn't amenable to scientific investigation because it precedes both the fourth dimension of space (time) and the laws of physics.

However, the current model doesn't explain why the universe has the unbelievably precise combination of fundamental physical constants necessary for the formation of stars, planets, and, ultimately, life itself. The odds of this happening by sheer chance is so fantastically small that some cosmologists, including Stephen Hawking, hypothesize that our world is part of a *multiverse* filled with universes, each having its own set of physical laws and at least one—ours—with just the right fine-tuning to allow us to be here pondering it.

I'm not alone in believing an unobservable, untestable idea is pretty small beer in the pantheon of "great scientific theories." The late mathematician and science writer Martin Gardner insisted there is not a shred of evidence that there is any universe other than the one we live in. Physicist Paul Davies concurs. He points out that "invoking an infinity of unseen universes to explain the unusual features we see in this one is just as ad hoc as invoking an unseen Creator." Each requires a leap of faith.

So . . . is the universe the ultimate free lunch? Could everything have sprung from nothing? If not, what was there before? Is there a creator who created himself? Maybe the origin of the universe is simply beyond our intellectual pay grade as a species. Perhaps human beings contemplating the riddle of existence are no different than a cat looking at a library or a dog observing an internal combustion engine. There is an explanation. But they're never going to know it.

Even more disturbing, could we live in a rational universe that rests on an irrational foundation? Are we forced to choose between an inexplicable God and the Absurd?

Everyone has his own favorite ideas on this subject, of course. (Encourage family and friends to hold forth and you may learn them.) But Holt warns us not to fall prey to the philosopher's fallacy, the tendency to mistake a failure of imagination for an insight into the way things really are.

He claims that existential thinkers tend to fall into one of three camps. *Optimists* hold that there has to be a reason for the world's existence and we may ultimately discover it. *Pessimists* believe there might be a reason for its existence, but we'll never know it. And *rejectionists* believe there can't be a reason for the world's existence and therefore the question itself is meaningless.

Even if the optimists are right, however, no one really believes science will ever explain *everything*. There will always be a place for philosophy, theology . . . and disputation. Science, for example, can't validate ethical truths. There will always be a gap between the scientific *is* and the ethical *ought*.

For now—and maybe forever—there are no ultimate explanations. There simply isn't a logical bridge from nothing to being. Or, as one wag put it, the universe is the answer. What we still don't know is the question.

It comes as no surprise, then, that neither Holt nor anyone he interviews offers a definitive answer to his question. But he does a fine job of summing up what we do know and how. In my view, he arrives at his best conclusion not at the end of the book but smack in the middle, on page 138:

Scientists can account for the organization of the physical universe. They can trace how the individual things and forces within it causally interact. They can shed light on how the universe has, in the course of history, evolved from one state to another. But when it comes to the ultimate origin of reality, they have nothing to say. This is an enigma best left to metaphysics, or to theology, or to poetic wonderment, or to silence.

A Requiem for an Atheist

Author Christopher Buckley called him "the greatest living essayist in the English language." Scientist Richard Dawkins praised him as "the finest orator of our time." Tony Blair said he "was a complete one-off, an amazing mixture of writer, journalist and polemicist . . . fearless in the pursuit of truth and any cause in which he believed."

So I was saddened to learn in June 2010 that British-born author and journalist Christopher Hitchens had been diagnosed with fourth-stage esophageal cancer. (As Hitchens himself was quick to point out, there is no stage five.)

A lifetime of drinking, smoking, and burning the candle at both ends had caught up with him. And it was a particularly harrowing diagnosis. "My father had died, and very swiftly too, of cancer of the esophagus," wrote Hitchens. "He was seventy-nine. I am sixty-one. In whatever kind of 'race' life may be, I have very abruptly become a finalist."

After 18 months of rigorous and painful treatment, he died. Yet the news was cheered in some quarters. You may know why. In addition to writing and lecturing widely on literature, history, poetry, politics, and current affairs, Hitchens was perhaps the world's most outspoken atheist. His book *God Is Not Great: How Religion Poisons Everything* was an international best seller.

It generated strong reactions in many quarters. In his last collection of essays, *Mortality*, Hitchens quotes one gleeful blogger:

> Is it just coincidence that out of any part of his body, Christopher Hitchens got cancer in the one part he used for blasphemy? Yeah, keep believing that, Atheists. He's going to writhe in agony and pain and wither away to nothing and then die a horrible agonizing death, and THEN comes the real fun, when he's sent to HELLFIRE forever to be tortured and set afire.

It's hard to read this without recalling the words of Mahatma Gandhi: "I like your Christ. I do not like your Christians. Your Christians are so unlike your Christ."

More typical, however, was the reaction—after Hitchens' death—of Francis Collins the director of the National Institutes of Health, the head of the Human Genome Project, and an evangelical: "I will miss Christopher. I will miss the brilliant turn of phrase, the good-natured banter, the wry sideways smile when he was about to make a remark that would make me laugh out loud."

Collins said his many public debates with Hitchens sharpened his own thinking about faith. "His knowledge of world religions was truly impressive—he had a much more detailed grasp of the Christian Bible than most Christians do." A close friend, Collins personally oversaw Hitchens's cancer treatment up to the very end.

Although I didn't know Hitchens well, I met him on several occasions and had the opportunity to chair a debate between him and Christian apologist Dinesh D'Souza at FreedomFest in Las Vegas in 2009.

Afterwards, we met for dinner at Le Cirque in Bellagio. That evening, Hitchens did something no dinner companion should ever get away with: For more than four hours, he dominated the conversation. Under almost any circumstances imaginable, this would be unpardonably boorish. Yet there were no objections. Hitchens spent the entire meal teasing, cajoling, challenging, toasting, and confronting everyone at the table.

In nineteenth-century London, those who knew him considered Oscar Wilde the greatest conversationalist ever. Hitchens was
the finest talker of our own era. Whenever he spoke, fully formed,
beautifully crafted sentences poured forth in that precise, well-
modulated British baritone, complete with literary references and
historical analogies.

Even his put-downs were subtle and witty. One friend at the
table took issue with one of Hitchens's observations and complained, "Well, I think such-and-such." Hitchens smiled gently, pat-
ted his hand, and said, "It's not what you think, my dear, it's *how*
you think." Then he was off on another topic.

Since I was having dinner with the world's foremost unbeliever,
I couldn't resist prodding him a little. "So Christopher, is there *anything* you consider spiritual?"

He thought for a moment. "If we were debating," he replied. "I
would say 'no, nothing.' Although I will concede the existence of
the noumenal, things inaccessible to our experience. "Then he
added, "Of course, some things are sacred."

"Really?" I said, surprised to hear his confession. "What?"

"The truth," he said without hesitation. "And life. Life is
sacred."

Hitchens did a lot of living in his too-short life. Unlike many
armchair polemicists, he was a tireless traveler. His journalistic
work took him to Northern Ireland, Greece, Cyprus, Portugal,
Spain, and Argentina in the 1970s, generally to shine a light on
entrenched dictators or other abusers of power. In the decades that
followed, he traveled throughout Eastern Europe and the Middle
East—and not without incident. He was shot at in Sarajevo, jailed
in Czechoslovakia, and, in 2008, beaten bloody in Beirut.

To inform and entertain his readers, he submitted to everything
from waterboarding to a bikini wax. (You can watch his short-lived
waterboarding experience on YouTube.) His conclusion?
Simulated drowning is torture. But a bikini wax is more painful.

Hitchens cultivated friendships with a long list of politicians,
scientists, celebrities, and power brokers. But he had a special fondness for fellow literary lions Martin Amis, Salman Rushdie, Julian

Barnes, James Fenton, Clive James, and Ian McEwan. The group liked to play a game in which members came up with the sentence least likely to be uttered by one of their number. Hitchens's winner was "I don't care how rich you are, I'm not coming to your party."

He was a true renaissance man, seldom produced an uninteresting sentence, and wrote with authority on everything from the rightful home of the Elgin Marbles (Greece) to the devotional poetry of Philip Larkin to short biographies of his heroes Thomas Paine, Thomas Jefferson, and George Orwell.

In the end, however, Hitchens was best known for his broadsides against religious (and particularly Islamic) fundamentalism. He blamed it for much of the world's violence, irrationality, bigotry, intolerance, racism, ethnic cleansing, subjugation of women, and denial of scientific progress.

He took issue with those who said a life without religion lacks hope or meaning: "A life that partakes even a little of friendship, love, irony, humor, parenthood, literature, and music, and the chance to take part in battles for the liberation of others cannot be called 'meaningless' except if the person living it elects to call it so."

Hitchens kept writing and produced some of his most poignant work after receiving his cancer diagnosis. Yet he never lapsed into sentimentality or self-pity, reminding readers that he was only doing rapidly what we all are doing slowly. And he kept passing along his insights:

> The stupendous importance of love, friendship and solidarity—has been made immensely more vivid to me by my recent experience. I can't hope to convey the full effect of the embraces and avowals, but I can perhaps offer a crumb of counsel. If there is anybody known to you who might benefit from a letter or a visit, do not *on any account* postpone the writing or the making of it. The difference made will almost certainly be more than you have calculated.

As the months went by, it became clearer that he was losing his battle with cancer and he confessed that it was becoming easier to misconstrue a friend or get unintentionally hurt. "People say—I'm in town Friday: will you be around? WHAT A QUESTION!"

Hitchens uttered and wrote a lot of provocative things during his career. His opinions—sometimes brilliant, often outrageous, always witty—were so diverse and far-ranging that no one could agree with them all. But he goaded his readers and listeners to think. Indeed, that was his only goal.

Hitchens insisted we should respect free inquiry, challenge ideas, suspect our own motives, avoid excuses, distrust anything that contradicts science or offends reason, fight all forms of tyranny (especially over the mind), picture all experts as "mammals," never be a spectator to unfairness or stupidity, and seek out argument and disputation for their own sake.

"Take the risk of thinking for yourself," Hitchens wrote. "Much more happiness, truth, beauty and wisdom will come to you that way."

THE NATION'S MOST MISUNDERSTOOD MAN

In 1776, the Declaration of Independence proclaimed that all men are created equal. Yet it took almost another century—and the bloodiest war in American history—to begin turning that promise into a reality.

I was reminded of this on a recent trip to the famous Gettysburg battlefield, site of the key turning point in the Civil War and the first major loss for General Robert E. Lee, commander of the Confederate Army of Northern Virginia and, in the eyes of some historians, the most misunderstood man in American history.

When the war broke out, Northern newspapers branded Lee, a distinguished officer who turned down Lincoln's offer to lead the Union army, a traitorous lowlife, a Benedict Arnold who believed one man could own another as he might own a horse or a set of dishes.

Yet the Civil War was not just about slavery. Abraham Lincoln, who failed to carry a single Southern or border state, campaigned on a platform of not interfering with slavery anywhere it was legal, even pledging to maintain it if it would preserve the Union. Not all slave states joined the Confederacy. And almost 90 percent of whites in the South did *not* own slaves.

The Civil War was also about states' rights. Many Southerners felt they were acting in the American tradition of liberty by asserting their independence and leaving the union. In his conversations and letters, Lee—a committed Christian—consistently condemned slavery as unnatural, ungodly, impractical, and morally abhorrent. Nor did he support the Southern states' right to secede, calling it "nothing less than a revolution."

So why did he turn down Lincoln's offer to lead Union forces? After all, this was America's highest field command, an opportunity to earn not just the president's gratitude but unparalleled reward and national glory. The answer can be found in Lee's deep Virginia roots. His father, "Light Horse" Harry Lee, was a Revolutionary War hero who fought beside George Washington and was later the state governor and a member of Congress. Yet when Harry defended a friend who published a newspaper opposing the War of 1812, he was attacked by a mob and nearly beaten to death. Disfigured and permanently disabled, he abandoned his wife and children for Barbados, leaving his son to raise his siblings and care for his invalid mother.

Robert was 11 at the time. He quickly learned how to handle responsibility, went on to graduate second in his class at West Point, and distinguished himself during the Mexican War in 1847. The American general in chief, Winfield Scott, said Lee was the finest soldier he ever served with.

Yet Lee would not raise a sword against his fellow Virginians. As the war approached, he resigned his commission in the U.S. Army to head the Virginia state militia, taking command of Confederate troops only after the state later voted to secede. And as general, Lee quickly demonstrated that he was a shrewd tactician and commander, winning numerous battles against larger, better-fed, and far better equipped Union forces.

Lee's reputation soon became the stuff of legend, as he inspired shoeless, starving soldiers to dig deep within themselves and fight beyond their endurance. At times, his Confederate soldiers marched barefoot through fallen snow, lived on cattle feed, and endured countless other privations. (My Gettysburg guide said

Union soldiers claimed they could smell Lee's troops before they heard them.)

His soldiers' devotion was due in part to the way Lee carried himself. He was always impeccably dressed and groomed, never swore, and exhibited superb posture and horsemanship. He was deeply, genuinely humble as well, never seeking adulation or applause or considering that he deserved them.

Lee fought and suffered with his men, always sharing their burdens and discomforts, wintering with his men during miserable field conditions, when any number of wealthy landowners would have been honored to host him.

Lee's troops followed him not out of fear or obligation but out of the greatest respect and admiration. And he returned their devotion, refusing near the war's end to risk a single man's life once he recognized the cause was lost. Lee's farewell address to the Army of Northern Virginia—sometimes referred to as "the Gettysburg Address of the South"—is one of the most poignant moments in American history.

The Civil War cost Lee almost everything. He lost his home, his career, his investments, and virtually all his worldly goods. He suffered the premature death of a daughter, a daughter-in-law, two grandchildren, and countless friends and family. He was deprived of his citizenship and liable to be tried for treason. Yet he never abandoned his personal standards or wavered from doing what he thought was right even in the face of devastating consequences.

Perhaps Lee's greatest service to the nation was his example after defeat. He believed it was his duty to make the best of circumstances, to help rebuild the South, and to convince Southerners to become a strong and vital part of the American Union.

He was unanimously elected president of struggling Washington College in Lexington, Virginia (now Washington and Lee University). Founded in 1749, the school had been nearly destroyed in the war and stood on the brink of collapse. Lee rebuilt it, expanded the curriculum, put the school on solid financial footing, and raised the enrollment eightfold. He also introduced the honor system. When a new arrival once asked for a copy of the school's rulebook, Lee explained, "We have but one rule here, and that is every student must be a gentleman."

There was no doubt that Lee himself was. He considered it a special honor to push his invalid wife in her wheelchair. During the war, he picked wildflowers between battles and pressed them into letters to his family. He once described two dozen little girls dressed in white at a birthday party as the most beautiful thing he'd ever seen.

Perhaps Lee's highest gift to subsequent generations was the example of his own character. He is a reminder that what ultimately matters is not what you have or how much you've accomplished but *who you are*. Lee dedicated himself to the ideals of honor, fortitude, forgiveness, and reconciliation.

Teddy Roosevelt cited Lee—along with George Washington—as one of the two all-time greatest Americans. Winston Churchill wrote that Lee was "one of the noblest Americans who ever lived, and one of the greatest captains known to the annals of war." In *Lee: A Life of Virtue*, biographer John Perry writes, "To know how he lived, what he thought, and what experiences and legacies defined his life is to know the essence of honor, sacrifice, faith, humility, and ultimate triumph in the face of defeat."

For some, of course, Lee will be forever tainted by the fact that he fought on the side of those who would preserve slavery and dissolve the Union. But if the poet Alexander Pope was right that "the proper study of mankind is man," it will always remain essential to understand not Robert E. Lee the general, the military tactician, or the educator, but Robert E. Lee *the man*.

Why Grant's Final Victory Was His Greatest

Having examined the character of Robert E. Lee, it seems only fair that I tell the story of his adversary Ulysses S. Grant, a nineteenth-century hero whose final victory may have been his greatest.

Born into meager circumstances in 1822, Grant was the eldest son of an Ohio leather tanner and shop clerk. It was not a warm and fuzzy childhood.

His mother showed a strange indifference to him, waiting six weeks after his birth to even name him. As a boy, he was small and awkward, and suffered from an inferiority complex. He struggled at school and was taunted by classmates. He had no talent or appreciation for music and claimed he was tone-deaf. Later in life he said, "I know two tunes. One is 'Yankee Doodle' and the other isn't."

His father was able to arrange an appointment to West Point, but Grant was not the model cadet. His dress, deportment, and appearance were slovenly. He collected demerits for tardiness and unsoldierly bearing. And while he was a fine equestrian, he showed little interest in military history or tactics.

He graduated without distinction, was passed over for promotion in the peacetime army, and floundered as a civilian. He failed at every attempt to make money and settled into life as a clerk in his father's store. He married a woman, Julia Dent, whose charms—by all accounts—were lost on everyone but Grant. Indeed, "plain" may have been a generous description of his short, dumpy, slightly wall-eyed bride, who in photographs appears entirely grim. Yet he remained devoted to her and their children his entire life.

Unfortunately, Grant was also devoted to whiskey. His fondness for white lightning made him the town drunk until the Civil War came along and saved him.

Unusual for a military leader, Grant detested war and recoiled at the sight of blood, even refusing to eat any meat aside from poultry. Yet military historians hail his genius. As a strategist, he benefited from a keen knowledge of maps and topography. A former quartermaster, he knew the supreme importance of supply lines. And he had discovered a gift for soldiering and composure under fire during the Mexican War (1846–1848). "There is no great sport in having bullets flying about one in every direction," he wrote Julia at the time. "But I find they have less horror when among them than when in anticipation."

Lincoln admired the way Grant fought and won, claiming the general held territory "like he had inherited it." But Grant also suffered numerous setbacks. His army was surprised at Shiloh, the most furious battle ever fought on American soil. (More Americans were killed there than in all previous American wars combined.) He lost nearly 7,000 men in a fruitless assault on Lee's entrenched lines at Cold Harbor. He bungled the Battle of the Crater in the siege of Petersburg. Yet his mistakes were never decisive, and his many successes earned him a well-deserved reputation as a brilliant and aggressive commander.

The dashing Robert E. Lee is rightly remembered as one of history's greatest generals. But we shouldn't forget it was Grant who beat him and set new standards of military honor with his gracious and generous treatment of Lee and his men at Appomattox Court House. (For the rest of his life, Lee never allowed a word against Grant to be spoken in his presence.)

After the war, Grant served two terms as president. Yet, in a world where speechmaking was popular entertainment and politicians routinely spoke for hours, Grant was largely silent. His presidency was less than inspiring, as well. The government was saddled with an enormous war debt. Huge parts of the country remained broken, starving and mired in catastrophic defeat. The South's economy was virtually destroyed. And Grant had the misfortune of presiding over America's first economic depression, including the Panic of 1873.

However, he was trusted in the South as well as the North. That made him the perfect figure to reunify the nation. As president, he also signed legislation that created the national park system, declared that the Indians required as much protection from the whites as the whites did from the Indians, and avoided foreign wars and entanglements. In short, Grant affirmed the integrity of American institutions and demonstrated decency, good intentions, and common sense.

Unfortunately, he had little understanding of money and no business sense whatsoever. In 1880, Ferdinand Ward, a 28-year-old con man and business associate of his son, Buck, invited the former president to become a partner in his Wall Street brokerage house. Grant, a trusting man who seldom bothered to read documents before signing them, agreed.

Before long, Ward reported stupendous profits and doled out generous amounts of cash to partners. Grant believed he was rich. But Ward was running a multimillion-dollar Ponzi scheme, and in 1884 it blew up, devastating investors and bankrupting Grant and his family. It was the most colossal swindle of the age.

In 1877 retiring presidents did not have the benefits they do today—no generous pension, no office and staff at government expense, no lucrative speaking engagements. The former president, who had blundered in every business opportunity, had nothing to fall back on.

Worse, he had recently been diagnosed with throat and mouth cancer, an incurable disease before the advent of radiation and chemotherapy. Grant knew he was beginning a slow and painful death, one that would leave his wife Julia not just penniless but deeply in debt.

Fortunately, his friend Mark Twain, the second most famous American of the day, offered to publish his memoirs, with a generous royalty agreement. Grant accepted, though he realized his poor health meant he had only a few months to complete the task.

Under overwhelming pressure, he wrote an astonishing 10,000 words a day. First he dictated them, but as he lost his ability to speak, he wrote them down by hand on a yellow legal pad. The writing was slow, laborious work. Yet he carefully figured out how much pain he could endure and how much morphine he could take before it clouded his mind and stopped his pen. Grant completed the massive work in a matter of months, finishing the last chapter three days before he died. On his deathbed, he was still struggling with the maps and proofs.

Grant did not have researchers, assistants, or draft writers. Yet his prose is clear and direct and demonstrates an amazing memory. The words that make up the two-volume work are his own. And they are exceptional.

Twain was astounded when he read the manuscript, claiming that there was not one literary man in a hundred who could furnish copy as clean as Grant's. He had offered to publish the memoirs because he assumed that the book would be a financial success. Now he saw its remarkable literary quality. "There is no higher literature than these modern, simple *Memoirs*," he said. "Their style is flawless . . . no man can improve upon it." Coming from the single greatest figure in American letters, this was high praise indeed.

The book was not just an immediate sensation—it was the biggest best seller in American history. Biographer Michael Korda notes that in the late 1800s, you could count on finding two books in every American home: the Bible and Grant's memoirs.

The book earned more than $450,000 in royalties, a sum worth nearly $10 million today, easily—to that point—the largest payment to an author in world history. Twain noted that if he paid the royalties in silver coin at $12 per pound, it would weigh over 17 tons. Yet the general never saw his book's success.

Thousands of carriages made up Grant's five-mile-long funeral procession. More than a million people, the largest crowd ever to gather on the North American continent, turned out to say good-bye. The *New York Times* reports that at one time his tomb in New York was a bigger tourist attraction than the Statue of Liberty.

Here was a genuine Horatio Alger story. Grant's early life was marked by failure, shame, and disappointment. Yet he rose to become the most famous and respected man in the nation. Grant won the Civil War and saved the Union, concluding it on a note of grace. His two terms as president were marked by peace abroad and reconciliation at home. He helped heal the nation's wounds and saved his family from financial ruin by writing a brilliant, landmark memoir, one of the most successful books in American literature, while dying and wracked with pain.

For these reasons, he deserves to live on in our memory. As Theodore Roosevelt said, Grant—like Washington and Lincoln—takes his place "among the great men of all nations, the great men of all time."

THE OTHER FREEDOM
DOCUMENT OF 1776

As every American kid learns in school, the history of the United States is the story of a political experiment that began with the Declaration of Independence. Yet, coincidentally, another set of documents—also published in 1776—helped launch a global economic miracle to rival the political one. I'm referring, of course, to Adam Smith's *Wealth of Nations*.

Smith (1723–1790) was a Scottish moral philosopher and leading Enlightenment thinker, and his magnum opus is rightly venerated. Historian Niall Ferguson calls *Wealth of Nations* and his earlier book *The Theory of Moral Sentiments* two of the foundational texts of Western civilization, setting them alongside the works of Isaac Newton, John Locke, Edmund Burke, and Charles Darwin.

To appreciate why the book had such an impact, you have to appreciate the nature of economic thinking at the time. Gold, land, and agricultural output were regarded as the only real "wealth." So the British government granted royal charters for monopolies, imposed protective tariffs on imported goods, and regarded trade as a zero-sum game among countries for an economic pie that could not be expanded.

Smith changed all this by exposing the flaws in the "mercantilist" view and demonstrating through reason, evidence, and powerful examples that:

- Competition ensures a steady fall in prices and a rise in the quality of goods.
- Specialization—the division of labor—leads to mutually beneficial collective knowledge and is the original source of economic growth, increased productivity, and greater prosperity. (It's the reason you don't have to build your home, repair your car, or pull your kids' teeth.) Self-sufficiency is poverty.
- Free trade creates pricing mechanisms that allow supply to meet demand. (No individual or group is wise enough to know or create *market prices*.)
- Any definition of liberty that is not based on property rights—including the right to keep the fruits of your labor—is meaningless.
- Government interference to protect favored groups hurts the interests of both businesses and consumers. (A lesson the folks in Washington never seem to learn.)

Smith's key insight, however, was that no external force, no coercion, no violation of freedom is necessary to produce economic cooperation. Free enterprise is about voluntary exchange for mutual benefit. Individuals, pursuing their own self-interest, are led, in his famous phrase, as if "by an invisible hand" to promote the public good, even though that is not their intention.

In their relentless quest for profits and market share, businesses innovate and improve efficiencies, creating products that are better, cheaper, or longer lasting. No one benefits more than the consumer. Yet most Americans still don't get it. It just seems intuitive that a bunch of committed, caring, well-intentioned people—let's call them public servants—making disinterested decisions on everyone's behalf should be able to create a better, fairer economic system than a bunch of unenlightened vendors grasping for profits.

But it simply isn't so. Just as Charles Darwin showed how complex design and ecological balance are unintended consequences of competition among organisms, Smith demonstrated how prosperity and social harmony are unintended consequences of completion among striving individuals. Both are designed from the bottom up, not the top down.

Unwittingly, millions of unconnected strangers cooperate to provide the products and services we want or need. In his essay "I, Pencil," Leonard Read (1898–1983), founder of the Foundation for Economic Education, illustrated how. There's nothing extraordinary about a pencil, a simple, everyday object made of wood, lead, metal, and rubber. Yet no single individual on earth can create one, or even knows how. Trees must be harvested. Wood must be cut, transported, and milled. The lead (actually graphite) must be mined, mixed with ammonium hydroxide, cut, dried, and baked. The wood receives six coats of lacquer, which requires growing castor beans and refining them into castor oil. The bit of metal, called the ferrule, is brass. That requires other laborers and craftsmen to mine zinc and copper and process them into sheets. The eraser is a rubber-like product made with rapeseed oil from the Dutch East Indies and sulfur chloride. These are just a few of the hundreds of steps necessary to create an ordinary pencil that sells for a fraction of a cent.

No one sitting in some central office orders these people around, commanding them to do their part to create the finished product. They live in different lands, speak different languages, practice different religions, and may even hate one another, yet they still cooperate without most of them even knowing that pencils are one of the end products of their labor. This is why Smith's book is sometimes referred to as the Declaration of Interdependence.

And it is a truly global phenomenon. In *The Rational Optimist*, Matt Ridley notes:

> In the two hours since I got out of bed I have showered in water heated by North Sea gas, shaved using an American razor running on electricity made from British coal, eaten a slice of bread made from French wheat, spread with New Zealand butter and Spanish marmalade, then brewed a cup of tea using leaves grown in Sri Lanka, dressed myself in clothes of Indian cotton and Australian wool, with shoes of Chinese leather and Malaysian rubber, and read a newspaper made from Finnish wood pulp and Chinese ink.

. . . Actually, I am guessing at the nationalities of some of these items, because it is almost impossible to define some of them as coming from any country, so diverse are their sources.

What inspires these creative human energies? How do millions of tiny "know-hows" naturally and spontaneously come together to meet our desire for an endless array of products and services? Smith provided us with the answer more than two centuries ago. Although he wrote before the Industrial Revolution, he recognized that prices emerging from voluntary transactions between buyers and sellers coordinate the activities of millions of people in such a way as to make everyone better off. It was a startling idea then and it remains one today: economic order emerges as the unintended consequence of the actions of many people, each seeking nothing more than to further his own interests.

Smith could not have imagined the technology, medicines, and standard of living that we enjoy today. Yet the *Wealth of Nations* describes exactly how it happens, how tens of millions in the private sector cooperate to meet our needs without any threat of force or coercion. We may know only a few hundred people in our entire lives, yet—thanks to the free market—great multitudes stand by at all times to serve and assist us.

Despite the innumerable benefits that accrue from others pursuing their own self-interest, plenty of reasonable, well-educated individuals complain that "it's a shame our economic system is based on selfishness" and "business owners put *profits* ahead of people." Yet no economic system based on anything other than self-interest has ever created anything like the material prosperity we enjoy today. There has never been an economic system based on national pride or economic equality or public-spiritedness that has ever worked. And the pursuit of profit benefits more than just customers and shareholders. Private enterprises that don't value key employees, for instance, will lose them to competitors. And there is a good reason business owners focus on the bottom line first. Without profits, there can be no employer-sponsored health benefits, no 401(k) plan, no paychecks, and no Christmas parties. Nor any corporate tax revenue to support our social-welfare system.

Economic self-interest doesn't drag us down. It raises us up. (As Smith put it, "Nobody ever saw a dog make a fair and deliberate exchange of one bone for another with another dog.") *The Wealth of Nations* is not a justification of amoral greed. Smith devoted most of his career to a single philosophical project: the betterment of life.

He avoided unworkable, utopian ideals and instead proposed solutions that tap into human imagination and ingenuity, those qualities that best promote happiness, liberty, and prosperity. His genius was to establish economics as a scientific discipline.

Because he didn't keep a diary, wrote few letters, and burned all his unpublished papers, we don't know much about Smith's personal life. However, we do know his favorite subject was mathematics, that he was a religious skeptic who never lost his faith in the power of economic freedom, and that he lived most of his life with the only woman he ever really loved—his mother.

He also enjoyed society and conversation, calling them "the most powerful remedies for restoring the mind and its tranquility." His best friend was the philosopher and historian David Hume, and he also associated with Edward Gibbon, Samuel Johnson, Sir Walter Scott, James Watt, Voltaire, Rousseau, Edmund Burke, and Benjamin Franklin. As P. J. O'Rourke writes, "It's impossible today to imagine knowing a range of such people. There are no such people."

In short, Smith's theories and conclusions are so fundamental to modern economics that we no longer appreciate their brilliance. He predicted that using our mental and physical capacities would make rulers as unnecessary and inconsequential as possible. He insisted that real prosperity, for nations as well as individuals, depended on income exceeding expenses. And he demonstrated that the best and sturdiest foundation for economic security is something we never find in short supply: rational self-interest.

THE RIGHT MAN AT THE RIGHT TIME

On the morning of April 4, 1968, Martin Luther King, Jr. slept late. In the afternoon, he joked with his companions, taunting them into a pillow fight in his motel room. An hour later, he stepped onto the balcony of his room and paused a second, debating inwardly whether to take a jacket. Somewhere off to his right, James Earl Ray brought the crosshairs of his rifle sights onto King's neck and squeezed the trigger.

It was the end of a life . . . and the beginning of a powerful legacy.

On the third Monday in January each year, millions of Americans pause to remember and celebrate the life and achievements of Martin Luther King, Jr., the twentieth century's most influential civil rights activist. King spoke passionately, wrote persuasively, and led countless marches and sit-ins, crying out for justice for oppressed minorities in the United States. In 1963, he was *Time* magazine's Man of the Year. The following year, he was awarded the Nobel Peace Prize at 35, the youngest Peace Prize winner ever. In 1977, he was posthumously awarded the Presidential Medal of Freedom, the nation's highest civilian honor.

Like Washington and Lincoln, King was unequivocally the right man in the right place at the right time. It wasn't just that blacks were systematically denied equal rights and opportunities. There were the daily humiliations as well.

As a boy in the Deep South, King was regularly shooed away from white stores, white restaurants, white bathrooms, even white water fountains. On a long return bus trip from a debating contest, he and his teacher were told to stand so that white passengers could sit. In a downtown department store, a matron once slapped him, complaining, "The little nigger stepped on my foot!"

King later recounted that he became determined to hate every white person. But his dad, a Christian minister, taught him otherwise, though he, too, chafed at the indignities. Once, after being pulled over by a traffic policeman, the officer addressed his father as "boy." Pointing to young Martin on the seat beside him, he snapped, "That's a boy. I'm a man."

On another occasion, the two were told by a shoe clerk that blacks could only be served in the rear of the store. His father grabbed the boy's hand. "We'll either buy shoes sitting here or we won't buy any shoes at all."

America was two societies, separate but unequal. Yet King became convinced that racial hatreds were driven not by individual convictions but by attitudes deeply ingrained in society. He made it his mission to change those attitudes. And he insisted it must be done without violence.

His commitment to peaceful change came from three primary sources. The first was the Gospel. The second was Henry David Thoreau's theory of nonviolence, famously articulated in his essay "On Civil Disobedience." The third was the nonviolent thoughts and actions of Mohandas Gandhi with his strikes, boycotts, and mass marches against British colonial rule.

Following these examples, King urged his followers to stand up to taunts, threats, and harassment—not to mention clubs, police dogs, and water cannons—with peaceful resistance. It wasn't easy. One evening, a bomb exploded on the front porch of his house, wrecking the front parlor. King rushed home to find his wife, Coretta, and their infant daughter safe in a back room. But the yard and street were filled with more than 300 angry blacks, many armed with guns and knives. Sirens wailed. Skirmishes with the authorities broke out. Reporters and onlookers pressed in, adding to the pandemonium.

Yet standing on the shattered glass and rubble of his front porch, King raised his hand and shouted, "We are not advocating violence! We must love our white brothers no matter what they do to us. Love them, and let them know you love them." To King, forgiveness was not an occasional act but a permanent attitude.

Today, he is best recognized for his civil rights activism, but the Baptist minister really fought for something more. His goal was nothing less than the moral reconstruction of American society.

He became an outspoken opponent of the war in Vietnam. Blacks were disproportionately serving and dying in the conflict, and in a television interview, Mike Douglas asked King whether his opposition to the war might be misinterpreted. King replied that he hoped not, since he opposed *any* American fighting and dying in a senseless war.

Watching film clips of Dr. King recently, I marveled again at his courage and intellect, his calm demeanor, his sense of hope. The civil rights leader insisted we all have an amazing potential for good, that there exists in each of us a natural identification with every other human being, and that when we diminish others, we diminish ourselves.

"The greatest tragedy," he declared, "is not the words and deeds of the so-called bad people, but the appalling silence of the so-called good people."

THE MOST POWERFUL THING YOU CAN DO FOR YOUR BODY

One of the most common practices found in the world's many spiritual traditions is fasting.

The Buddha refrained from food and drink during his period of asceticism, and Buddhist monks fast on the new moon and full moon each month. Fasting is an integral part of the Hindu religion. And abstaining from food and drink from sunup to sundown during Ramadan is one of the Five Pillars of Islam.

The Bible contains dozens of references to fasting. It is prescribed as preparation for an important event (Judges 20:26, I Samuel 14:24), as a mourning rite (II Samuel 1:12, 12:16–23), and as a form of atonement (Jonah 3:5, Jeremiah 36:9). In the New Testament, Jesus fasts for 40 days. In the Old Testament, Moses does (twice).

Orthodox Jews fast during Yom Kippur, Tzom Gedaliah, and Purim. Early Christians fasted every Wednesday and Friday. Many do today during Advent, Pentecost, the Assumption, or Lent.

In March 1799, President John Adams even called for a national day of fasting, proclaiming that the foundations of all religious, moral, and social obligations were being steadily undermined and, in quite Presbyterian-sounding language, calling on the American people to repent. (It was Adams who later repented, however, convinced that this tactical error cost him his reelection.)

For skeptics, fasting evokes some of the worst associations with religion: irrationality, guilt, self-denial, or punishment. But practitioners contend it is a way of purifying and recharging. Fasting strengthens temperance and self-control. It can be a time to focus on your inner life rather than your physical needs. And it promotes humility and empathy. After all, is it not easier to identify with the plight of the world's hungry when your own stomach is rumbling?

Now science is trumpeting the benefits of fasting as well. Research shows that nothing is more effective in increasing human life span than caloric restriction. But during fasting periods, the body also kicks into repair mode, fixing and protecting tissues, organs, and the nervous system. And it can lead to a powerful sense of catharsis, especially for those who have overindulged in processed or unhealthy foods.

In short, this ancient spiritual practice is gaining millions of secular adherents today. Why? Because the scientific evidence in favor of it is unequivocal. Just ask Dr. Michael Mosley.

Mosley trained as a doctor at the Royal Free Hospital in London but, after passing his medical exams, joined the BBC and began making science documentaries. He has won numerous awards, including being named Medical Journalist of the Year by the British Medical Association. His 2012 documentary *Eat, Fast and Live Longer*, viewed by more than 30 million people worldwide, has become something of a sensation.

Dr. Mosley insists there is nothing else you can do for your body that is as positive and powerful as fasting. He points to mountains of evidence—and his own personal experience—to prove it.

Fasting doesn't have to mean giving up food for an entire day. Dr. Mosley's recommended technique is *intermittent fasting*. He recommends consuming a quarter of your regular calorie intake on two nonconsecutive days each week. That's 600 calories for men and 500 for women. For obvious reasons, it's called a 5:2 Diet: five days on and two off.

But calling it a "diet" is a misnomer, really. Diets are about what you eat. Intermittent fasting is about *not eating*. With this plan, there are no complicated rules to follow, no recipes to learn, no points to add up, and no lists of foods you can or can't consume. Instead of saying "no" all the time, you get to have a life. You can plan ahead and still enjoy yourself at parties, cookouts, and banquets. You get to eat all the foods you enjoy most of the time.

And there are numerous health benefits. Studies indicate that intermittent fasting:

- Improves your cholesterol count and blood glucose levels.
- Moves you closer to a body mass index of 25 or less, reducing your risk of high blood pressure, type 2 diabetes, coronary heart disease, strokes, gallbladder disease, colon and breast cancer, osteoarthritis, and respiratory problems.
- Improves IGF-1, a hormone that prevents cell death and slows the aging process, reducing the risk of a number of age-related diseases.
- Switches on millions of repair genes in response to the minor physiological stress of fasting.
- Gives your pancreas a rest, boosting the effectiveness of the insulin it produces.
- Promotes an enhanced sense of well-being. Many fasters report a "glow," perhaps the result of something going on at a metabolic level that governs our moods.

Scientists hypothesize that intermittent fasting is beneficial because human beings evolved in an environment where food was often scarce. We are the product of hundreds of thousands of years of feast or famine. Intermittent fasting mimics the environment in which our bodies and genes were shaped.

Your body is exquisitely adapted to respond to stresses and shocks in a way that makes it tougher and healthier. (The scientific term is *hormesis*.) When you severely restrict your calorie intake, you "fool" your body into believing it is in a potential famine situation. It switches from its ordinary "go-go" mode to a maintenance mode. And that leads to a cornucopia of health benefits.

Intermittent fasters generally make some unexpected discoveries. They find they commonly eat not because they're hungry but because they're bored, thirsty, or just because food happens to be in front of them. We eat from habit, or because it's a certain hour, or because we are afraid that if we don't we will be hungry later.

There are a number of common misperceptions about fasting. The first is that it is incredibly difficult. You might imagine that hunger builds and builds until it becomes unendurable and you find yourself face down in the local pizza buffet. The reality is that hunger comes and goes in waves, then passes.

We tend to assume that fasting makes it harder to concentrate. Yet fasters report that it sharpens their senses and concentration. Most believe fasting will make them irritable. But studies show it improves mood and protects the brain from dementia and cognitive decline.

Of course, the biggest misperception is that if you fast one day you'll just blow it by pigging out the next. Yet study participants told to eat all they want on nonfast days regularly report eating only slightly more than they ordinarily do.

The biggest obstacle to fasting is fear. Our brains evolved to persuade us to eat as much as we can as often as we can to guard against future hunger. That was an effective strategy in a food-deprived environment. But in our modern world of inexpensive, easy-to-access, fatty, salty, and sweetened foods, it's a decided handicap.

If you'd like to give fasting a go, you might begin by watching Dr. Mosley's documentary, widely available on the Internet. In a follow-up book, he also offers these tips:

- Find a friend or family member to join you . . . or at least support you in your endeavor.
- Which two days you fast each week are unimportant, any two nonconsecutive days will do. But for scheduling reasons, many find that Mondays and Thursdays work best.

- Try fasting from 2 to 2. Most daily fasts are from morning until night. But they needn't be. Any 24-hour period will do. You may find it easier to fast, say, from 2 P.M. one day until 2 P.M. the next.
- When tempted to eat, always wait 10 or 15 minutes to see if the hunger subsides.
- Stay hydrated. You can be tempted to eat when you are only thirsty.
- Distract yourself, if necessary, with a walk, a phone call, or anything that takes your mind off eating. As fasting advocate Brad Pilon notes, "No one's hungry the first few seconds of a sky dive."
- Prep your fast-day food in advance. This keeps you from the dangerous temptation of foraging in the panty or fridge.
- Whatever you eat on a fast day, relish it. Go slow.

Many describe fasting as the equivalent of hitting a reset button for your entire body. You may fear that going an entire day while consuming 600 calories or less is sheer torture. But anyone who has had to prep for a colonoscopy knows that a day without eating is hardly the end of the world.

Mosley reports that men enjoy intermittent fasting because it is uncomplicated, requires no cooking skills, and can be viewed as a challenging but enjoyable test of willpower. Women tend to like it because it's easy to implement, their bodies respond to it rapidly, and while they may not be eating their beloved chocolate today, they know they will be tomorrow.

Intermittent fasting is not an invitation to binge and starve. It is calibrated and sensible. Over time most fasters see their appetite moderate. And while it may seem like a tough slog at first, over time the sense of deprivation diminishes and eating this way becomes second nature.

Not everyone should fast, of course. The list includes children, pregnant women, people with underlying medical conditions, or those who are already too thin.

But for the rest of us, there are good reasons to give it a try: a self-repairing physiology, greater disease resistance, a cognitive boost, and improved longevity. And, not least of all, steady and sustainable weight loss. Dr. Mosley reports that he dropped pounds so rapidly that he switched to fasting just one day a week once he reached his ideal weight.

In short, intermittent fasting offers a host of physical and psychological benefits. It is not a diet but a sustainable strategy for a longer, healthier life. You stand to gain a lot . . . and perhaps lose quite a bit, as well.

THE "HOWLING ATHEIST" WHO GOVERNED THE COUNTRY

"Make your own Bible," Ralph Waldo Emerson proclaimed in his *Journal* in 1836. "Select and collect all the words and sentences that in all your readings have been to you like the blast of a trumpet."

He meant to encourage readers to follow the Renaissance practice of compiling favorite quotes, poems, letters, passages, and aphorisms into a Commonplace Book to be used for reflection and inspiration. But, while Emerson didn't realize it at the time, Thomas Jefferson took this idea quite literally more than 30 years earlier.

In February 1804, President Jefferson sat in the White House with two copies of the King James Bible, a razor, a pair of scissors, and a pot of glue. He was about to do something that would have shocked and outraged his contemporaries.

Jefferson believed that centuries of translation and transmission had left the Gospels with imperfect texts and contradictory dictates that left readers with a jealous and angry deity, magic and superstition, some deplorable ethical standards, and embarrassing theological notions.

So he began cutting and pasting onto blank pages—in English, French, Greek, and Latin—those verses of Matthew, Mark, Luke, and John that he believed were supported by history, science, and common sense.

He fashioned a chronological story of the life of Jesus of Nazareth and his teachings. It included the Sermon on the Mount, the most memorable parables, and the admonitions to help the poor and love your enemies. It left out Jesus walking on the Sea of Galilee, turning water into wine, and feeding the multitudes with two fish and five loaves of bread. Jefferson struck out all the miracles, genealogy, and prophecy, and excised every passage "of vulgar ignorance, of things impossible, or superstitions, fanaticisms, and fabrications." Out went the angels, the virgin birth, and the resurrection.

Jefferson was confident in his project, telling his friend John Adams that he found the true parts "as easily distinguishable as diamonds in a dunghill." On March 10, he completed his 46-page volume, *The Life and Morals of Jesus of Nazareth.*

Jefferson was a lifelong student of religion. One biographer calls him "the most self-consciously theological of all American presidents." Yet he also was a great admirer of empiricists like Isaac Newton, John Locke, Francis Bacon, David Hume, and the mighty Voltaire.

He had incredibly wide interests. Jefferson was a statesman, historian, surveyor, philosopher, scientist, diplomat, architect, inventor, educator, lawyer, farmer, breeder, manufacturer, botanist, horticulturalist, anthropologist, meteorologist, astronomer, paleontologist, lexicologist, linguist, ethnologist, biblicist, mathematician, geographer, librarian, bibliophile, classicist, scholar, bibliographer, translator, writer, editor, musician, gastronome, and connoisseur of wine.

It's hard to reflect on Jefferson's life without feeling like a bit of an underachiever.

But he was also a man of contradictions. He wrote the Declaration of Independence but was a lifelong slaveholder. He insisted life in the public spotlight did not suit him, but served as delegate to the Virginia General Assembly and to Congress, as governor of Virginia, minister to France, secretary of state, vice president, and president from 1801 to 1809. He was an advocate of strictly limited government but doubled the size of the United States with a swift purchase of the Louisiana Territory that many claimed was unconstitutional.

Jefferson was an autodidact, an avid reader in English, Spanish, French, Greek, and Latin. His personal library, which later became the foundation of the Library of Congress, contained nearly 10,000 volumes. Many of these dealt with ethics and morality.

However, Jefferson insisted most religious doctrines served merely to prop up clergymen or those in power—recall that the king of England ruled *by divine right*—and prevented people from understanding the straightforward message of Jesus. He believed that obedience to the teachings of the Nazarene and reflection on the purity of his life would help citizens transcend their parochialisms and narrow self-interests.

In 1777, Jefferson composed the Virginia Statute for Religious Freedom, enacted a few years later by the Virginia House of Delegates. It was the first law in the history of the world to guarantee freedom of worship, protecting people of all faiths and those with no religion at all.

Jefferson himself was at least nominally Episcopalian. He was raised in the Church of England at a time when it was the established church in Virginia. He was christened in an Anglican ceremony and married by an Anglican priest. But his religious skepticism began at an early age. He questioned, for instance, why the creator of the universe would reveal himself solely to a small population in the eastern Mediterranean and leave the rest of the world in a spiritual void, ignorant of his existence.

Although he kept his personal beliefs private, Jefferson often spoke out against religious intolerance. In his *Notes on the State of Virginia*, first published in 1784, he argued that unorthodox beliefs and outright disbelief posed no threat to society. "It does me no injury for my neighbor to say there are twenty gods or no God. It neither picks my pocket nor breaks my leg."

For this, Jefferson was denounced in the election of 1800 as an arch-infidel and a "howling atheist." New England ministers warned that, if elected, Jefferson would confiscate all Bibles and convert churches into temples of prostitution.

Hurt by these attacks on his integrity and character, Jefferson chose not to respond in public, but in a letter to his friend Benjamin Rush he wrote, "They believe that any portion of power confided to me will be exerted in opposition to their schemes. And they believe rightly; for I have sworn upon the altar of God, eternal hostility against every form of tyranny over the mind of man."

Jefferson insisted that mystical revelations could not satisfy his questions. Only reason and evidence were reliable guides to an understanding of life and the natural world. He cast a skeptical eye on everything that smacked of superstition or the supernatural.

Jefferson's bible was and is heretical to many. But it was the only form of Christianity he could embrace. Though he rejected the notion of revelation, he was not anti-religious. He found poetry in the Psalms, love in the Gospels, and beauty in the Anglican hymns and liturgy.

Jesus himself wrote nothing, of course. And Jefferson felt his teachings had suffered badly at the hands of his editors. In particular, he believed that the apostle Paul was "the first corruptor of the doctrines of Jesus," turning the religion *of* Jesus into a religion *about* Jesus. This, in his view, led to fanciful tales, dogma, and what he called "priestcraft." Jefferson wanted to rescue Jesus from these distortions.

In his bible, he compiled the passages he believed were truthful to reveal a master whose "system of morality was the most benevolent and sublime . . . ever taught, and consequently more perfect than those of the ancient philosophers."

Jefferson credited Socrates, Epicurus, Pythagoras, Cicero, Seneca, Epictetus, and others with teaching followers to govern their passions. But he considered their views on our duties to each other to be sorely underdeveloped. He concluded that Jesus's precepts were "the most pure, benevolent, and sublime which have ever been preached to man," calling him the greatest moral philosopher and "the first of human Sages."

While he showed *The Life and Morals of Jesus of Nazareth* to a few close friends, the book—which he had bound in red leather with gold embossing by a Richmond bookbinder—was never published during his lifetime. It served only as his private manual of devotion.

Today, Jefferson is variously described as an agnostic, a Deist, a skeptic, a Unitarian, or a freethinker. But in another letter to Rush he wrote, "I am a Christian, in the only sense he wished any one to be; sincerely attached to his doctrines, in preference to all others; ascribing to himself every human excellence; and believing he never claimed any other."

The Jefferson Bible, recently on display at the Smithsonian's National Museum of American History and available for viewing online, is a book that has intrigued and outraged Americans ever since it was published by the National Museum in Washington in 1895.

For Jefferson, the subject of religion was fascinating, alarming, enraging, and inspiring. He blithely predicted near the end of his life that reason would ultimately prevail and every young man in the country then living would die a Unitarian. He was spectacularly wrong about that, of course. But millions of educated Americans, Christian and Jewish and of no particular congregation, now hold similar views.

Jefferson was a champion of the primacy of reason and individual conscience, the cause of human rights, and the importance of education. He not only defined his own time but still shapes our understanding of freedom today.

In the Declaration of Independence, Jefferson declared that the American Republic was founded on universal principles. That meant they were decidedly for export.

So were his views on individual conscience. For Jefferson, the greatest of all liberties is the freedom of the human mind.

PART THREE

A WEALTH OF UNDERSTANDING

As a young man, I believed patience—to the extent I thought about it all—was overrated as a virtue.

When opportunities arise, you jump. When conditions change, you adapt. When problems crop up—as they always do—you tackle them promptly. Being patient, I thought, was a great way to get left behind. Most in the business world would probably agree.

However, patience can also be a powerful asset and, occasionally, an indispensable one. It creates endurance, offers strength in trying circumstances, and encourages us to give time a chance to work its magic. Saint Augustine called patience "the companion of wisdom." Not long ago, my good friend and colleague Dave Fessler reminded me why.

On a trip to Nicaragua in 2012, Dave went body surfing at the beach. But a Pacific wave picked him up and slammed him into the ocean bottom headfirst, leaving him paralyzed below the neck and floating face down. Fortunately, a couple of buddies in the surf recognized his plight and pulled him to shore. He was medivacked to Hospital Metropolitano in Managua and given an MRI, then flown back to the States where he underwent surgery on his spinal column.

Today, Dave is recuperating at home and undergoing rigorous physical therapy. On a recent visit, I found him resting comfortably and in good spirits. His doctors are pleased with his physical progress, too. But Dave knows his convalescence will be arduous, painful, and measured in years. He has limited mobility and is still unable to get out of bed. That means his smiling wife, Ann, who should be first in line for canonization, feeds him, bathes him, brushes his teeth, and does everything—including scratching his nose—that an incapacitated person requires.

One evening, over a scrumptious home-cooked dinner of green beans, mashed potatoes, and marinated venison, Dave offered up something I wasn't expecting. "I'm actually really lucky."

Looking at him lying there in his neck brace, I felt my own problems shrivel up and die. "How so?" I asked.

"When the doctor reviewed my MRI in Managua, he said my spinal column was completely severed. So I was lying there thinking, 'That's it. I'm going to be a quadriplegic for the rest of my life.' Half an hour later, another doctor walked in the room and begins apologizing. So now I'm thinking, 'What fresh hell is this?' But to my surprise, he tells me the prior doctor had misread my MRI. I had a severe contusion, but my spine was only bruised not broken. I could be a lot worse off today."

His plight would be tough on anyone, but perhaps especially for someone as active as Dave. He was an avid outdoorsman, a hunter and fly-fisherman who routinely rode his mountain bike 150 miles a week. And he can build or fix just about anything. For the past several years, he had been busy living out his dream, renovating the old Pennsylvania farmhouse where he and his family now live. Dave did the plumbing, electrical work, woodwork, drywall, painting, and landscaping. He even installed the slate roof. When I mentored Dave as a financial writer a few years ago, he said he wished he could write like me. I told him I wished I could do everything else like him.

Dave's physical toughness is a great aid to his convalescence. But so is his mental toughness. He has plenty of struggles ahead of him, and there are no guarantees. Recovery from an injury like his is not a linear progression. Improvements come in fits and starts. He knows he may not recover all his sensory or motor functions. Yet not once since the accident have I heard him moan and complain or lapse into self-pity. I told him I wasn't just impressed but inspired.

The remaining essays in this book are about other people and ideas I found inspirational. In a world where we all struggle and suffer to some extent—some, like Dave, far more than others—it's always refreshing to encounter a book, a movie, a play, a concert, or an individual that provides a positive spark or insight. We shouldn't neglect one of the greatest assets in our rich cultural inheritance: a wealth of understanding

Why You Love and Need the Rat Race

When I was young and worked dreary, low-paying jobs, I often imagined that one day I might be independently wealthy and spend my days playing golf, taking a dip in the pool, and then relaxing and shooting the breeze with a few buddies.

I now know myself well enough to realize that a string of days spent this way would be profoundly boring, if not a living hell. I have to be working on something, knocking out goals, achieving things. You may feel the same way. I know Todd Bucholz does.

Bucholz is a former director of White House economic policy, an award-winning Harvard professor, a former director of the top-performing Tiger Hedge Fund and the author of several books, including *Rush: Why You Love and Need the Rat Race*.

At an investment conference a few years ago, I moderated a debate between Bucholz and economist, author, and investment adviser Mark Skousen.

Comedian Lily Tomlin once noted that the trouble with the rat race is that even if you win, you're still a rat. But Bucholz has a different take. He points out that we are free men and women living in a free society and contending in a free market. The rat race—our capitalist system—is a good thing. It not only creates unparalleled innovation and prosperity, it also gives our lives meaning and direction.

Most of us have a deep need to strive and to create. Work makes us feel like we are expending our energy in productive ways. You earn not just the respect of others but self-respect. After all, self-esteem is not a default position. You earn it by doing something worthy of esteem.

Success—or the pursuit of it—validates your life. It gives you a reason to get out of bed in the morning. It makes you feel that just maybe you really are worth all the love and attention your parents lavished on you. And it makes us feel good. Neuroscientists report that challenges light up your left prefrontal cortex and give you a rush. Competition—for love . . . for knowledge . . . for achievement . . . for financial security—ignites our passions, releases dopamine, and delivers a natural high. It is when we are competing that we learn, grow, and feel most alive.

Social scientist Arthur Brooks points out that people who are out of work, as more than 14 million Americans are today, have a 16 percent greater chance of having felt "inconsolably sad" at some point in the prior month.

Sure, competition creates stress and anxiety. But then, almost everything worth achieving does. Stress is the salt of life. We feel exhilaration from mastering anxiety, not avoiding it. Conquer your fear of flying or public speaking, for example, and new worlds will open up for you.

We were not made to sit around like poached eggs on toast, contemplating our navels and pondering the nature of existence. We are programmed to take risks, to exercise our talents. A life of engagement kindles your brain and gives you energy. It builds stamina and fortitude. It provides the spark of life.

If you are retired or out of work, there are still plenty of opportunities. Studies show that people who give their time to charity are up to 45 percent more likely to describe themselves as "very happy."

In a meritocracy like ours, of course, earned income is closely aligned with education. Those with college degrees generally earn more than those with high school diplomas. Those with postgraduate degrees earn more than those with bachelor degrees. But those with more education also work more hours than those with less. And the self-employed, it turns out, work more than anyone else. Consequently, the preponderance of wealthy Americans are professionals or business owners who put in more than 50 hours a week. But, for many of them, money isn't the primary motivator.

Last year I hiked a 10-mile leg of the Appalachian Trail with my friend John Mackey, CEO of Whole Foods. John's salary is one dollar a year. ("And the company hasn't paid me the last five years," he told me. "They still owe me five bucks!") He receives no bonuses. And he donates his annual stock options to the Whole Planet Foundation, a nonprofit organization that helps the world's poor achieve dignity and prosperity through micro-credit (and competition).

John doesn't have to work, and he has plenty of outside interests to keep him busy. So why does he deal with all the hassles and challenges of running a Fortune 500 business? Because he loves it.

Most of the rest of us are engaged in our work, too. Bucholz points out that a random sample of over 27,000 Americans between 1972 and 2006 showed that 86 percent of us were satisfied with our jobs, with nearly half describing themselves as "very satisfied."

Work—the so-called rat race—tests and refreshes our mental circuits. It gives our lives purpose and direction. The paycheck is further validation that our time is well spent. And the desire to improve our lives, help our families, and give to worthy causes are all honorable motivations.

How about the other side? Didn't Skousen muster any valid arguments *against* the rat race? Indeed, he did. We'll turn to his arguments, based on the work of Aristotle, next.

How to Live the "Good Life"

What does it mean to live a good life? What is true happiness? How much is enough? And how can you make the best use of the years you have remaining?

Aristotle asked these important questions more than 2,000 years ago. Bucholz and Skousen tried to answer them from two different perspectives. Bucholz argued that our ultra-competitive capitalist system is a blessing, responsible for breakthrough technologies, lifesaving medical advances, and widespread material prosperity. Yes, the rat race can create stress and anxiety, but it also gets our juices flowing, sharpens our minds, and helps give our lives purpose and direction.

There is a potential risk, however. It is easy to become obsessive about work and its financial rewards—and to wake up one day and find that the life you're leading is about as deep as a candy dish. Skousen pointed out that a life well lived is not about getting and spending. We have to make time for family, friends, laughter, and leisure. It's about balance and moderation. Aristotle called it the *golden mean*. Understand its importance and you're on your way to the good life. But first a little background . . .

Aristotle (384 B.C.–322 B.C.) was a student of Plato and tutor to Alexander the Great. He taught logic, rhetoric, metaphysics, poetry, music, and ethics. He introduced a structure of logical thought that laid the groundwork for empirical science. And his writings became the first comprehensive system of Western philosophy.

Yes, the world today looks very different from ancient Greece. But people themselves haven't changed a whit. Then, as now, the conventional view was that a "successful" life is about career advancement, power, prestige, material goods, sensual pleasure, and social approval. Aristotle rejected this line of thinking and devoted his life to exploring the best way for human beings to live.

He insisted that genuine happiness isn't about fulfilling our wants and needs. (Even animals do that.) For reasoning, morally aware beings like ourselves, happiness is the result of something that sounds quaint (even old-fashioned) in our do-your-own-thing society: virtue.

Only the virtuous life, Aristotle said, leads to real satisfaction. And virtue can be found in the middle, between the extremes of excess and deficiency. He gave examples:

Deficiency (Vice)	Balance (Virtue)	Excess (Vice)
Cowardliness	Courage	Recklessness
Dishonorableness	High-mindedness	Vanity
Timidity	Confidence	Arrogance
Indifference	Concern	Anger
Humorlessness	Wit	Buffoonery
Asceticism	Temperance	Gluttony
Miserliness	Generosity	Wastefulness
Slothfulness	Fitness	Fanaticism
Churlishness	Friendliness	Obsequiousness
Unkindness	Magnanimity	Pride
Hopelessness	Faith	Zealotry
Ignorance	Wisdom	Pedantry
Abasement	Humility	Narcissism

In almost every area of our lives, including the rat race, disproportion is the thief of real happiness. Even good things—wealth, love, friendship—pursued immoderately, can become a source of misery. The trick is to find the right balance.

I've found that this "middle road" leads to success in the investment arena, too. For example, many investors are so risk averse they find themselves in ultra-low-yielding investments that make it impossible to reach their financial goals or beat inflation. Others roll the dice and lose their shirts in options, futures, penny stocks, or other speculative vehicles. The solution is not to fear risk or ignore it, but rather to embrace and intelligently *manage it*.

Always look for that *golden mean*, the middle ground between too much and too little. This is what leads to real satisfaction and contentment, to what Aristotle called *eudaimonia*. Recognizing these virtues is one thing, of course. Embodying them is another. "It is no easy task to find the middle," Aristotle conceded. But if we don't, our lives will be "full of regrets."

People are often drawn to Aristotle's ideas in the second half of life. By then, most of us have set aside our youthful fantasies about money and celebrity and are focused instead on knowledge, awareness, companionship, and community. Plus, you've gained something you didn't have before: perspective.

Aristotle's natural audience is mature, thoughtful people who have a healthy dissatisfaction with their current lives. They want to feel that they are not just living but *flourishing*. That requires wisdom. And the highest wisdom, in Aristotle's view, is to care about *the right sorts of things*: other people, truth, freedom, justice—in short, virtue.

In this debate, Bucholz and Skousen both made valid points. Meaningful work, whether you're compensated for it or not, is an essential part of the good life. But so are decent health, human connections, personal goals, and a wealth of interests. Aristotle would offer that work is the virtue between the excesses of idleness and frivolity. But he would also remind you that to be human is to realize your potential for growth, to develop your higher aspects.

Happiness, he declared, isn't something you feel. It's something you do.

NASSIM NICHOLAS TALEB . . . AND THE PURSUIT OF PHRONESIS

Dr. Nassim Nicholas Taleb is the best-selling author of *Fooled by Randomness*, a book about the underestimation of randomness in modern life, and *The Black Swan*, a book about the likelihood of major, unpredictable events occurring in financial markets. (With auspicious timing, the latter came out just as the financial crisis of 2007–2008 began to unfold.) Both books are now considered investment classics.

Taleb is an insightful and unorthodox thinker. A practitioner of mathematical finance, he is an Oxford University professor, a former hedge fund manager, and a scientific adviser at Universa Investments. When I last chatted with him, he told me he was writing a book about religion. More recently, he published *The Bed of Procrustes*, a collection of philosophical thoughts about work, life, and the limits of human understanding.

Taleb believes that when facing situations where we have limited knowledge, we tend to squeeze our thinking into widely accepted ideas and prepackaged narratives, with potentially explosive consequences.

Many of Taleb's points are counterintuitive. Some are maddening. Virtually all are thought provoking. That alone makes him worth reading. Here is a sampling of his gems:

- Education makes the wise slightly wiser, but it makes the fool vastly more dangerous.
- Work destroys your soul by stealthily invading your brain during the hours not officially spent working.
- Preoccupation with efficacy is the main obstacle to a poetic, noble, elegant, robust, and heroic life.
- They will envy you for your success, for your wealth, for your intelligence, for your looks, for your status—but rarely for your wisdom.
- Don't cross a river because it is on average four feet deep.
- Asking science to explain life and vital matters is equivalent to asking a grammarian to explain poetry.
- Those who think religion is about "belief" don't understand religion, and don't understand belief. By accepting the sacred, you reinvent religion.
- After a long diet from the media, I came to realize that there is nothing that's not (clumsily) trying to sell you something. I only trust my library.
- The opposite of success isn't failure; it's name dropping.
- Read nothing from the past 100 years; drink nothing from the past 4,000 years (just wine and water).
- In Aristotle's Nicomachean Ethics, the *magnificent* is the "great-souled" who thinks of himself as worthy of great things and, aware of his own position in life, abides by a certain system of ethics that excludes pettiness. . . . The weak shows his strength and hides his weaknesses; the magnificent exhibits his weaknesses like ornaments.
- You will be civilized on the day you can spend a long period doing nothing, learning nothing, and improving nothing, without feeling the slightest amount of guilt.
- You are rich if and only if the money you refuse tastes better than the money you accept.

- It is as difficult to change someone's opinions as it is to change his tastes.
- Your reputation is harmed the most by what you say to defend it.
- There are two types of people: those who try to win and those who try to win arguments. They are never the same.
- My only measure of success is how much time you have to kill.
- Older people are most beautiful when they have what is lacking in the young: poise, erudition, wisdom, phronesis, and the absence of agitation.
- We are only truly alive in those moments when we improvise; no schedule, just small surprises and stimuli from the environment.
- You need to keep reminding yourself of the obvious: charm lies in the unsaid, the unwritten, and the undisplayed. It takes mastery to control silence.
- The sucker's trap is when you focus on what you know and what others don't know, rather than the reverse.
- "Wealthy" is meaningless and has no robust absolute measure; use instead the subtractive measure "unwealth," that is, the difference between what you have and what you would like to have.

More than anything, the book is an eloquent plea to slow down, think, and reconsider. Indeed, Taleb provides no commentary on any of his short sayings. His intention is not to explain but to provoke.

The author insists that an aphorism is like poetry, something that the reader needs to deal with by himself. Personally, I could spend hours thinking about these. But incorporating them would be better still.

■ THE GIFT A MAN GIVES HIMSELF

Years ago, when my daughter Hannah was much younger, she developed an unfortunate habit, one not unusual in kids. When she found herself in a situation where she had to choose between telling the uncomfortable truth or making up a lie, she'd opt for the latter.

I clamped down hard on this, but—as parents generally find—in many instances it simply isn't possible to know whether your child is telling the truth. You don't want them to think you don't trust them. But neither do you want them to believe they can escape the consequences, either immediate or long-term, of lost credibility.

I told her that the problem with a lie isn't just that it won't be believed. It's that *it will be.* Then the liar supposes that whenever he gets into a tight spot all he has to do is concoct something good and he can avoid the consequences of his actions.

But Abraham Lincoln was right. You can't fool all of the people all of the time. Eventually, the truth will out. And when it does, you're saddled with the reputation of being someone who can't be believed, even when you're telling the truth. It's a terrible thing, I told Hannah, to go through life knowing in your heart of hearts that you aren't the kind of person who can be trusted. What a sad opinion to hold about yourself, how damaging to your own self-image.

Yet this lesson was apparently lost on Russell Wasendorf, Sr. His story would be more shocking if it weren't becoming depressingly familiar. Wasendorf, the head of Peregrine Financial Group, admitted to embezzling more than $100 million from clients over nearly 20 years by personally doctoring bank statements and duping auditors with the help of a post office drop box.

A signed statement found in Wasendorf's car after his attempted suicide said, in part, "I have committed fraud . . . I had no access to additional capital and I was forced into a difficult decision. Should I go out of business or cheat? I guess my ego was too big to admit failure, so I cheated."

Let's be clear. The problem here wasn't too much pride but too little. How could Wasendorf walk around each day smiling at customers, slapping backs, and shaking hands—presenting himself as an economic success story—when he knew his life was a fraud?

This is clearly a man in denial, as further evidenced by his statement that, despite his private jet and $100,000 wine collection, "I did not live lavishly."

Some may point out that Wasendorf still takes a backseat to scoundrel supreme Bernie Madoff, who lived high on the hog while bilking his clients out of more than $64 billion, even stealing $15.2 million from the charitable foundation of Holocaust survivor Elie Wiesel.

What is wrong with these men? How could they show their faces in public knowing what they were doing in private? It's not just that they had no shame. They had no genuine self-esteem.

Psychologist Nathaniel Branden writes:

> One of the greatest self-deceptions is to tell oneself, "Only I will know." Only I know I am a liar; only I will know I deal unethically with people who trust me; only I will know I have no intention of honoring my promise. The implication is that *my judgment is unimportant and that only the judgment of others counts.* But when it comes to matters of self-esteem, I have more to fear from my own judgment than from anyone else's. In the inner courtroom of my mind, mine is the only judgment that counts. My ego, the "I" at the center of my consciousness, is the judge from whom there is no escape. I can avoid people who have learned the humiliating truth about me. I cannot avoid myself.

The other sure conclusion is that these men had no sense of honor. Some, like author and social commentator James Bowman, even claim that—outside the culture of the military—we are living today in "a post-honor society."

Let's hope not. Who we are, both as individuals and as a society, still depends on what we do and what we are willing to stand up for. Do we treat others fairly? Do we speak respectfully? Do we carry ourselves with dignity? Do we act with courage and personal responsibility? Few questions are more crucial than these—or are more important in determining the arc of our lives.

In the award-wining historical drama *Rob Roy*, Liam Neeson plays the title character, a man chided for his uncompromising and often inconvenient integrity. Asked in one scene by his young sons to define honor, his answer couldn't be more succinct. "Honor," he replies, "is the gift a man gives himself."

It's too bad Bernie Madoff and Russell Wasendorf never offered it to themselves. And now everybody knows it.

A Billionaire's Best Advice

If you had invested $10,000 in the S&P 500 in May 1965, when Warren Buffett took the helm of Berkshire Hathaway, and reinvested the dividends, it would be worth approximately $800,000 today.

Not bad. But if you had invested the same amount in Berkshire itself, your $10,000 would have grown to more than $64 million.

What is Buffett's secret? According to his business partner, the plainspoken Charlie Munger (who calls himself Berkshire's "assistant cult leader"), Buffett spends at least half his waking hours "just sitting on his ass and reading."

A billionaire in his own right, Munger spends much of his time the same way. Although he graduated from Harvard Law School, he describes himself as self-educated. The key to success in life, both financial and otherwise, he insists is "Elementary, Worldly Wisdom."

What is that, exactly? Munger believes we should all strive to improve ourselves by persistent reading of science, philosophy, religion, history, and literature. This allows you to think broadly and systematically and build a latticework in your head, a mental model of reality drawn from many disciplines.

Unfortunately, we live in a society that increasingly values specialization over breadth. We study to learn how to make a living, not how to make a life.

At his commencement address at USC Law School in 2007, Munger declared:

> Wisdom acquisition is a moral duty . . . I constantly see people rise in life who are not the smartest, sometimes not even the most diligent, but they are learning machines. They go to bed every night a little wiser than when they got up, and boy does that help, particularly when you have a long run ahead of you. . . . Nothing has served me better in my long life than continuous learning.

Few of us are fortunate enough to live surrounded by worldly philosophers and financial geniuses. Moreover, newspapers and magazines are so full of fresh trivialities that the quest to become well informed may actually prevent us from becoming educated. So we turn to books.

The goal is not to collect information but to gain understanding. How do you know you're on the right track? A good sign is when what you read forces you to stop, think, consider, and reread for clarification.

The benefits are profound. Deep reading increases your knowledge, but it also enhances your view of the world. It sharpens your critical thinking skills. And the process is unending. To become wiser, you need only be passionate to understand.

Time is limited, of course, while knowledge is limitless. To become even moderately well read may seem overwhelming. So we must become discriminating readers. Recognize that the vast majority of books (not to mention blogs and websites) are not worth your time. And the best books—with the exception of fields like science, medicine, and technology—are rarely the newest ones.

If you're looking for a place to start, you could do worse than to pick up a copy of *The New Lifetime Reading Plan*, a generous guide to history's greatest masterpieces. Simple perusing isn't enough, of course. You have to be an active reader, analyzing what you read, evaluating its worth, and either rejecting it or incorporating it into your worldview. It's important, too, to occasionally read authors with whom you profoundly disagree. If you don't, you'll end up simply confirming your biases. "One should recognize reality, even when one doesn't like it," says Munger. "Indeed, especially when one doesn't like it."

I have discussed mainly nonfiction here, but imaginative literature is also helpful. In "A Scandal in Bohemia," a puzzled Dr. Watson asks Sherlock Holmes, "What do you imagine that it means?"

Holmes replies, "I have no data yet. It is a capital mistake to theorize before one has data. Insensibly one begins to twist facts to suit theories, instead of theories to suit facts." That's a neat description of how a careful analysis begins.

Books are the carriers of civilization, allowing us to build a broader context around our thinking. It is chiefly through these volumes that we engage with superior minds. And they provide a priceless service: the opportunity to exchange error for truth. As Munger said, "In my whole life, I have known no wise people (over a broad subject matter) who didn't read all the time—none, zero."

Good readers become better thinkers. Good thinkers, in turn, make better investors, better workers, better spouses, better parents, better friends, better citizens, better human beings.

It's a good reason to visit the university on your shelf . . . or your local bookseller or library. As an ancient proverb tells us, a book is a garden carried in the pocket.

The Lost Art of Conversation

When Hannah reached age 13, she concluded that being popular at school was only slightly less important than breathing.

The problem is, like most of us at her age, she was more than a little shy, self-conscious, and socially awkward. Despite being an A-student, for instance, virtually everything she encountered was "cool" or "awesome" and little more. Her reluctance to express herself more effectively made it tough to reach out to new friends. So I tried to tell her something about the lost art of conversation.

For most of human history, face-to-face communication was the core of our interaction. Not today. We text, we e-mail, we blog, we friend each other on social networks. In the new age of electronic media, family and friends *converse* less than ever. As a result, we miss out on one of life's singular pleasures: a relaxed, civilized exchange of views.

Conversation offers infinite possibilities. It is great for polishing thoughts and generating new ones. It is unbeatable for beating the blues or forging friendships. The ultimate bond of all personal relationships—whether in business, friendship, or marriage—is conversation.

Yet two opposing attitudes pull us away from it. The first is the mistaken belief that it is unnecessary. Why bother making the call or the visit when you can fire off an e-mail? Unfortunately, text has difficulty conveying tone, the most important aspect of any communication. And think how much is conveyed with a smile, a glance, a wink, an eye roll, or an arched eyebrow. You really can't compare it with :), can you?

The opposite attitude is that conversation is too much work. So we don't really try. As we stare blankly into our electronic screens, the art of personal interaction is dying. Yet, as I told Hannah, there are good reasons to exercise our conversational skills.

Society provides lavish rewards to those who express themselves well. (Studies show that no single factor better predicts your future income than the size of your vocabulary.) Good talkers routinely ace the interview, get the contract, close the deal, win the girl. Get on with others and you will get on in life—and enjoy it more.

There is a widespread misconception that the best conversationalists are the smoothest talkers. Not so. (Indeed, glib talk generally comes off as phony or insincere.) And few of us will ever display the conversational genius of, say, Oscar Wilde, whose legendary wit captivated the salons of London.

Conversation is not meant to be a performance art or a competition, but an opportunity for mutual appreciation. And the best conversationalists are not the best talkers. They are the best listeners. History's wisest men and women have always known this:

Never speak of yourself to others; make them talk about themselves instead. Therein lies the whole art of pleasing. Everyone knows it and everyone forgets it.

—Edmond de Goncourt

The great gift of conversation lies less in displaying it ourselves than in drawing it out in others. He who leaves your company pleased with himself and his own cleverness is perfectly well pleased with you.

—Jean de la Bruyere

A gossip is one who talks to you about others; a bore is one who talks to you about himself; and a brilliant conversationalist is one who talks to you about yourself.

—Lisa Kirk

It is never necessary to try to impress your conversation partner. You can achieve that simply by demonstrating that they are worth the investment of time and attention it takes to find out what they are about.

It only takes a bit of curiosity. The idea is to find out more about the other person's attitudes, interests, nature, and disposition. For too many, however, a verbal exchange is not talking and listening but rather talking and waiting to talk again. You don't learn much that way. Or score many points.

Some insist they are poor conversationalists because they are introverted or tongue-tied. In some cases, that may be true. But those who struggle may be trying too hard to say the right thing. Far more important is not succumbing to the temptation to say the wrong thing.

A few years ago, I was invited to a small dinner party at a well-known director's home in Telluride. The filmmaker, who was a liberal (big surprise), made some innocuous comment about Bill Clinton. A Wall Streeter at the table, a conservative (another shocker), made a snarky comment in return. That caused our host to defend his view. This, in turn, drew support or rebuttal from various guests. In an instant, the verbal spitballs were flying. It was over in a few minutes, but by then it was too late. A pall set over the table. What was about to be an ideal dinner party with interesting people and fabulous food in a gorgeous setting became instead a tense, strained affair. The group never recovered the *joie de vivre* that had existed only moments before.

Don't get me wrong. Politics and religion can be fascinating subjects when open-minded friends are interested in a forthright exchange of views (although, in my experience, even these can be dicey). But in a social setting? Consider the likelihood that no one cares what you think. Good conversation is about drawing out the other, not delivering a monologue or a position statement.

The truth is that we are seldom better than our conversation. What you choose to talk about—and how you choose to say it—lays you bare. Every time you open your mouth, your mind parades alongside your words. That doesn't mean your conversation needs to be sparkling and original. Nor does it need to have a purpose or a point. Quite the opposite, in fact. The best conversations ramble. They have no predestination. It is all about the rhythm and flow.

In sum, good conversation is one of life's most accessible pleasures. It connects us to one another, forges friendships, increases social esteem, raises our mood, generates goodwill, enhances our information, and completes our education. And while prices rise and time shrinks, it is a luxury that remains free to us all.

True, conversation won't make you richer, thinner, or save your life. But it may save your marriage. As Charles Dickens said, "Never close your lips to those whom you have opened your heart."

So, as I explained to Hannah, value heartfelt conversation. Prioritize it. And reap the many benefits of a companionable, convivial life.

A VISIT EVERYONE SHOULD MAKE

On a recent family visit to Washington, D.C., my kids insisted on visiting the Bureau of Engraving and Printing so they could watch sheets of hundred-dollar bills roll off the presses and get stacked high. When we arrived, however, we discovered that the next tour wouldn't begin for almost an hour. A queue was beginning to form outside. Since it was cold and windy, I suggested we visit the U.S. Holocaust Memorial Museum next door.

"No, Dad, please," my daughter Hannah pleaded. "We've already been to the Lincoln Memorial, the National Archives, and the National Portraits Gallery. We've had enough history."

"Too depressing for a family vacation," my wife Karen chimed in.

But I exercised my veto override, arguing that we might actually learn something and, besides, it beat spending the next hour shivering in line. And so my frowning and reluctant clan trooped in—and experienced an emotional wallop we later agreed was the most unforgettable part of the trip.

The murder of two thirds of European Jews during the Second World War was so momentous an event that we are still coming to grips with it. We haven't yet grasped its full significance. Filled with artifacts, photographs, exhibits, and archival footage that both fascinate and terrify, the Memorial Museum is both a reminder of the horrors of genocide, wherever it occurs, and a call to stand up against hatred and injustice.

With each passing day, of course, there are fewer World War II veterans and Holocaust survivors to share their personal stories. And too few of us read history. But thanks in part to dramatic films like *Sophie's Choice, Schindler's List, Life Is Beautiful*, and *The Boy in the Striped Pajamas*, the story remains lodged in our collective conscience. And the basic facts never lose their ability to shock and overwhelm. . . .

The Holocaust began after Adolf Hitler came to power in 1933. Persecution began with an official boycott of Jewish-run businesses. Nuremberg Laws later stripped German Jews of their citizenship and prohibited their marriage to non-Jews. Other laws excluded them from parks and other public areas, fired them from civil service jobs, and required them to register their property (a necessary step before confiscation).

In 1939, the Nazis ordered the Jews to wear a yellow Star of David so that they could be easily recognized and targeted. As the Second World War began, they were ordered to live in "ghettos," restricted areas in big cities. At first, Jews could venture out during the day, so long as they observed curfew. But before long, leaving was prohibited.

Next came the deportations. Jews were loaded into train cars without food, water, ventilation, or a toilet and sent to concentration camps or death camps. Many, especially children, died of suffocation en route. Survivors were imprisoned, given tiny rations, and required to do hard physical labor. Torture was common.

Nazi doctors often conducted medical experiments on prisoners against their will. In one case, Josef Mengele—known as "the angel of death"—sewed together two four-year-olds at the back in an attempt to "create" Siamese twins. In another experiment, newborn babies were taken away from nursing mothers to see how long they could survive without feeding.

Some prisoners died a slow, agonizing death from disease or starvation. Others collapsed during brutal marches or forced labor. Most were exterminated, ruthlessly and efficiently. Sometimes German troops would shoot prisoners at the edge of a ravine, then cover them quickly with dirt, burying the wounded along with the dead. Millions of others were gassed with carbon monoxide or the insecticide Zyklon B. After gold fillings were extracted, the corpses were thrown into ovens and burned.

In *Night*, Auschwitz survivor Elie Wiesel, a Nobel Peace Prize recipient, wrote, "Never shall I forget the little faces of the children, whose bodies I saw turned into wreaths of smoke beneath a silent blue sky. Never shall I forget those flames that consumed my faith forever."

When General Dwight Eisenhower discovered the Ohrdruf concentration camp, he ordered every American solider in the area who was not on the front lines to visit it, so they "would know what they were fighting against." He also required the citizens of the nearby town of Gotha to tour it. After the mayor and his wife did, they went home and hanged themselves.

(On my last trip to Munich, I toured the Dachau concentration camp, easily the bleakest, most dispiriting place I've ever visited. Walking alongside the creek outside the crematorium, you wonder how even now the flowers blossom and the birds sing.)

An estimated 11 million people were killed during the Holocaust. Approximately 6 million were Jews. (More than a million were children.) The rest were "gypsies," homosexuals, the mentally and physically handicapped, and various "enemies of the state."

Almost as shocking as the crimes was the inaction of so many bystanders. Martin Niemoller, a Lutheran minister and early Nazi supporter who was later imprisoned for opposing Hitler's regime, wrote:

First they came for the socialists, and I did not speak out—
  because I was not a socialist.
  Then they came for the trade unionists, and I did not speak out —
  because I was not a trade unionist.
  Then they came for the Jews, and I did not speak out—
  because I was not a Jew.
  Then they came for me—and there was no one left to speak
  for me.

The U.S. memorial museum has a special children's exhibit, "Daniel's Story," that depicts the Holocaust through the eyes of an 11-year-old boy. First you visit his comfortable German home, complete with skis and soccer ball. Next you pass through his stark accommodations in the ghetto, with all its privations. You end up in his cramped, filthy quarters at the camp, where prisoners slept three or more to a bunk without mattress, sheets, or pillow.

I had tried to prepare my 9-year-old son, David, for what he was about to see, but after drinking it in, his face was a ball of confusion. Finally, he looked up and said, "Dad, why would anyone do this *to a kid?*"

I wish I had an answer.

The Man Who Made Dreams Come True

Browsing the newsstand at the local airport, I picked up a copy of *National Geographic Adventure*. It wasn't the splashy colors or the teasers on the cover that caught my attention. It was the magazine's tagline: *Dream it. Plan it. Do it.*

If life had an instruction manual, this might be the perfect six-word encapsulation. Yet as we grow older, we often find that important dreams remain unrealized, even achievable ones. Why is this? Maybe it's because we haven't really defined what it is we want or haven't devoted the time necessary. Or perhaps we haven't appreciated the importance of that essential step between dreaming and doing: planning.

One man who devoted his life to helping others clarify and realize their dreams was Dr. Stephen Covey, an educator, businessman and author of several books, including the mega-bestseller *The Seven Habits of Highly Effective People.*

Covey insisted that a rich, rewarding life is the result of striving toward worthwhile goals. And he made it his life's mission to show others how to achieve them. Born in Salt Lake City, it was while serving as a missionary for the Mormon Church that Covey discovered a talent and passion for teaching. And what he taught, primarily, was principle-centered leadership.

He asked readers to examine their lives to see if their actions were in harmony with their values, with universal principles. How are you treating people? What are you contributing on a daily basis? Are you doing good, or are you merely doing well?

The Seven Habits—and its even better follow-up, *First Things First*—is essential reading for achievers everywhere. Not just managers and business owners, but athletes, musicians, artists, and students. In *The Seven Habits*, Covey proposes that you:

- *Be proactive. Make things happen* rather than waiting for them to happen.
- *Begin with the end in mind.* Motivate yourself and direct your energy and activities more effectively by clearly defining and visualizing your goals.
- *Put first things first.* Eliminate time wasters (like mindless talk, channel surfing, and social networking) and focus on things that will improve the quality of your personal and professional life.
- *Think win-win.* You achieve things more easily in a cooperative effort than in a competitive struggle. Instead of thinking "their way" or "my way," look for how others can achieve their objectives as you realize yours.
- *Seek first to understand, then to be understood.* Persuasive communication is essential. But it begins with being an empathetic listener. Most people do not listen to understand; they listen with the intent to reply.
- *Synergize.* Ally yourself with capable individuals. Their strengths will compensate for your weaknesses and move you closer to your goal.
- *Sharpen the saw.* Balance all four aspects of your life—mental, physical, emotional, and spiritual—to become more effective. Sharpening the saw means renewing yourself through family, friends, exercise, and devotion or meditation.

These points are only a beginning guideline. Covey also offers concrete strategies for goal attainment. For instance, if, like so many, you are overwhelmed by everything on your plate, you might try this daily approach:

- Each morning, set aside 15 minutes to plan your day. Begin by making a task list that includes everything you need to do, from important things like making the presentation at work to more trivial matters like cleaning out the guest bedroom closet.
- After you've listed everything, label each item with an A, B, or C. A stands for "Must Be Done." B means "Should Be Done." And C is "Could Be Done."
- Return to the A's and number each task according to how vital it is. An action toward your most important goal (whether its career advancement, better fitness, or learning to play the clarinet) should always be ranked A1. Your second biggest priority is A2. And so on. Rank the B's and C's the same way.
- Then kick off each day by spending at least 30 minutes tackling A1. When your work is completed (or you've done all you can for one day), turn your attention to A2. And continue down the line. Only after all the A's are finished should you turn to the B's, and only when those are completed do you start on C1.

You won't get everything done on your list each day. Maybe you're so busy you don't get to the B's at all. And that's fine. But at least you're working on what matters most. (As Covey puts it, "The main thing is to keep the main thing the main thing.")

Carry the undone items over to tomorrow. Begin that day with another 15-minute planning session and a new master list—and then start your day by going hand-to-hand with A1.

You may think that—in your head at least—you're already doing something like this. But that's really not likely. Sitting down each morning to review your goals and write out a daily plan is enormously efficient. (And, trust me, at some point you'd rather clean out the closet than carry it forward one more day.)

Covey's real contribution was not efficiency techniques or time management strategies. It was urging us to focus on the important, not just the urgent. He reminds us that there shouldn't be a gap between what you value and how you spend your time. And he returns again and again to first principles, which always appeal to an educated conscience. That, too, takes effort, however. As he writes in *First Things First*:

> It actually takes more discipline, sacrifice and wisdom to develop an educated conscience than it does to become a great sculptor, golfer, surgeon, Braille reader, or concert pianist. But the rewards are far greater—an educated conscience impacts every aspect of our lives. We can educate our conscience by:
>
> - Reading and pondering over the wisdom literature of the ages to broaden our awareness of true north principles that run as common themes throughout time
> - Standing apart from and learning from our own experience
> - Carefully observing the experience of others
> - Taking time to be still, listen to and respond to that deep inner voice

Sadly, Dr. Covey died of complications from injuries he sustained in a bicycle accident in 2011. In his obituary, family members didn't dwell on his wealth, his fame, or his many accomplishments. They noted that he enjoyed cherry-chocolate malts, inspiring movies, practical jokes, and "letting the kids build peanut butter and jelly sandwiches on his bald head."

"We're here," said Covey, "to live, to love, to laugh, to learn, and to leave a legacy." Schedules are important. Efficiency is great. But our real focus should be principle-centered living. That is the means *and the end*, the journey *and the destination*.

Culled from the world's great religions and secular philosophies, Covey's principles offer a unique advantage. They allow you to work on the one thing over which you truly have control—yourself.

How to Talk Politics without Committing Murder

A buddy of mine recently confided that his wife and he are at daggers drawn. He openly questions whether their marriage will last. The problem isn't money, infidelity, drugs, alcohol, or anything like that. Their issue is that he is a dyed-in-the-wool liberal—as they both were when they married 25 years ago—but she has since become much more conservative.

"Now, whenever we talk politics," he said, "our voices rise, my blood pressure spikes, and the Yorkshire hides under the couch. God only knows what the neighbors think."

He's hardly alone. Who among us hasn't seen a social occasion degenerate into an intellectual food fight when politics rears its head? As a result, many hosts have an ironclad rule: no religion or politics at the table. You can hardly blame them. Yet it's a shame in some ways, since few subjects—under the right circumstances—are capable of provoking more stimulating or animated discussions.

"That's the problem," my wife, Karen, insists. "You *prefer* a provocative discussion. Why don't you just ask about people's kids like everyone else?"

She has a point. Too many are unable to talk politics without getting to the point where they're coughing up bile. As I see it, there are two reasons these "discussions" generate such supercharged emotions:

1. *Political views represent core values.* When someone disagrees with your politics, it's easy to construe it as an attack on what you hold most dear. That might be freedom, fairness, equality, or personal responsibility. Foundational principles like these are tough to compromise. And when uncompromising attitudes collide, sparks will fly.

2. *Politics is often about self-interest.* You might be unaware how close to home your "theoretical" discussion is hitting. More than a century ago, Ambrose Bierce defined politics as "a strife of interests masquerading as a contest of principles." You can spend years studying and debating whether a particular policy is good for the nation. But most voters know immediately and reflexively whether and how it benefits them personally. No one wants to appear selfish or ignoble, however, so we tend to characterize policies that counter our interests as unjust, unworkable, or just plain wrongheaded.

Given these high hurdles, how do you have a civil exchange with someone holding an opposite view? As a lifelong political junkie, I've pondered this for years and eventually came up with Seven Ground Rules for Political Discussion. Feel free to give them a try. Here are the terms of engagement:

1. You and your partner (or opponent, if you prefer) agree *not* to use the words *Republican, Democrat, conservative,* or *liberal,* or to mention the name of any living politician. This prevents the conversation from devolving into an emotional rant against a particular party or candidate.

2. Agree to use a level voice and normal tone, the kind you'd use to talk about last week's weather.

3. Agree that your mutual goal is to hear and understand your partner's point of view, not to change it. (A tough condition for proselytizers.)

4. To begin, your partner takes approximately five minutes to describe a particular policy he favors or opposes and why.

(It could be raising taxes, privatizing Social Security, withdrawing U.S. troops from the Middle East, or whatever.) Sticking to a single topic keeps the discussion from becoming unfocused.

5. When your partner's five minutes are up, you make no statement that confirms or contradicts his point of view. Instead, you take a few minutes to ask nonjudgmental questions that allow him to clarify his position and his reasoning.

6. Your partner then repeats steps 4 and 5 so you can voice your point of view on the same subject.

7. Afterwards, you take a few minutes to summarize what you do and don't agree on and why. Assuming a first-aid kit wasn't necessary, you can then move on to another policy position.

If you have the patience—or the temperament—to do this, you'll learn that those with opposing views aren't necessarily as "idiotic" or "ridiculous" as you may have assumed. Granted, the objective here is modest. It's not to defeat your partner with verbal jujitsu, point out the error of his ways, or change his party affiliation. (Trust me. It's a big enough victory just to hear "I see your point.") The idea is to have a forthright exchange of views, increase your understanding of him or her, and vice versa.

Of course, this all presumes that you want to talk politics and are willing to keep your side of the bargain. Even then, a couple of disclaimers:

1. Some of your fellow citizens, including many with the most ardent views, are not particularly well informed. Polls show that most Americans can't name their congressman or any members of the Supreme Court. They confuse the Declaration of Independence with the Constitution, have only the foggiest notion of the size of the federal budget deficit, and think foreign aid is a huge part of discretionary spending. As Winston Churchill noted, the best argument against democracy is a five-minute conversation with the average voter.

2. Don't waste your time arguing with anyone whose opinion you don't respect. This is doubly true when the person you're dealing with is a zealot. You have better things to do than bang your head against the wall. Ideally, you want to converse with someone who knows more than you on a particular subject and can inform and enlighten your own point of view.

You might reasonably ask how much success I've had using my Seven Ground Rules. Some, I'd say. Things can still get passionate, but a civil exchange *is* possible.

On the other hand, it really is a lot easier just asking about other people's kids.

THE TRUE SECRET OF SUCCESS

Each year for the past two decades, I made a weight goal as one of my New Year's resolutions. The same one, in fact. With each passing year, however, I only drifted a little farther from it.

Then something happened. I went on a plant-based diet, ran and lifted weights nearly every day, lost over 20 pounds, and got in the best shape I've been in in decades. The weight I'd been trying to lose for years, I lost in just 90 days—and that was well over a year ago. According to Professor Roberta Anding, a registered dietitian and director of sports medicine at Baylor College of Medicine, I am now at my ideal weight.

The continual challenge, of course, is maintaining it. But I really don't think I'll relapse. I've discovered that *fit feels better than anything tastes.*

The weird part is that losing the weight wasn't that hard. I just took two bad habits—sedentary activity and mindless eating—and replaced them with better ones, something I could just as easily have done any time in the past 20 years but for whatever reason didn't.

Habits govern our lives more than we acknowledge. A research study published in 2006 found that more than 40 percent of our daily actions are not decisions at all but habits. It's easy to fall into thoughtless routines and travel the same cow path through the day, throughout our lives even.

Why do we do this? Scientists say it is because the brain is constantly looking for ways to save energy and effort. It tries to make any routine into a habit as a way of ramping down. Beginning early in childhood, we develop a series of conditioned responses that lead us to react automatically and unthinkingly in most situations.

As a result, we tend to engage in the same activities, talk to the same people, eat the same foods, and do things the same old way. Yet our habits—what we say to our kids each night, whether we save or spend, how we organize our work routines, and whether we exercise—have an enormous impact on our health, productivity, financial security, and happiness.

Our lives don't change until we do. That happens when we move beyond dreaming, thinking, wishing, and planning and start *doing* something about it each day. Research suggests that the best way to get rid of an old habit is to replace it with a new and better one. When you get that familiar urge, you can reach for an apple instead of a Danish, head for the gym instead of the bar, turn on The Learning Channel instead of The Shopping Network. You override a bad habit by ingraining a new one. Experts say it generally takes about three weeks of consistent application for a new behavior to become routine.

Drastic action isn't required. Life is really a series of constant, tiny choices. Some call them *microactions*. They are the difference between doing nothing and moving forward. Microactions are small but they are not insignificant because they get you moving. And they compound. Over time, a series of regular, constructive actions creates a tipping point. Small changes in behavior ultimately create monumental differences in our lives.

There are plenty of microactions you could take *right now* to improve your life, your health, and your relationships. You could read 30 pages of a good book, take a walk, drink an extra glass of water, or call an old friend. Every time you complete a positive task, no matter how small, your brain gets an instant jolt of dopamine. This reward reinforces your behavior and helps cement the new habit.

I'm not suggesting that transforming a bad habit, especially a long-standing one, is necessarily quick or easy or simple. But with commitment, follow-through, and daily action, it *is* possible. For example, business success generally goes to individuals who make a habit of getting to work a little earlier or staying a little later, who apply themselves a little longer. Investment success accrues to individuals who develop a habit of saving before spending and who have the discipline to stick with proven principles of wealth creation.

Need some help? According to author and life coach Brian Tracy, there are seven essential steps to developing a new habit:

1. *Make a firm decision.* If you decide to exercise each morning, for example, when your alarm goes off, immediately get up and put on your exercise clothes. Don't give yourself an opportunity to procrastinate.
2. *Never allow an exception.* Excuses and rationalizations destroy new habits in their infancy. Perform the new behavior religiously until it becomes automatic.
3. *Tell others.* You become more disciplined and determined when you know others are watching to see if you have the willpower to follow through.
4. *Visualize your behavior.* Imagine yourself acting as though you already have the new habit.
5. *Create an affirmation.* Mental repetition increases compliance. Tell yourself something like "I get up and get moving immediately at 6:00 each morning."
6. *Resolve to persist.* Keep at it until you reach the point where it actually feels uncomfortable not doing what you promised you'd do.
7. *Reward yourself.* Rewards reinforce behavior. You begin to associate the pleasure of the payoff with the new actions themselves.

Just as your good habits are responsible for most of the success and satisfaction you enjoy today, your bad habits are responsible for most of your problems and frustrations. Most of us—deep inside—already know how to change this. It requires little more than transferring the discipline we already exercise in one part of our lives to some other part. For instance, you probably have friends or family members who are extremely disciplined about what they eat and drink but are completely undisciplined in their saving and spending habits, or vice versa.

Our natures are the same. It is our habits that separate us. Changing them allows you to take control of your destiny, overcome procrastination, revitalize relationships, achieve your ambitions, or obtain financial independence.

Real success is rarely the result of some one-time decision or a single herculean effort. It is regular, sustained, positive behavior that creates lasting change. As Aristotle observed a few thousand years ago, "We are what we repeatedly do. Excellence, then, is not an act, but a habit."

And if you stick with it, like me you might finally get a chance to make a new resolution.

How to Be a
Big Loser

My last essay about habits—and how changing two of my bad ones allowed me to reach my ideal weight in a few short months—provoked an outpouring of letters from readers asking for specific details.

I'd like nothing better than to unveil some unique, heretofore undiscovered weight-loss secret, but keep your seat. For starters, I lost only about 10 percent of my body weight, hardly an Olympian achievement. And I did it—stifle that yawn—by eating better, drinking less, and exercising more.

My reluctance to embrace a healthier regimen sooner was mainly due to ignorance and apathy. That changed, as I described earlier in the book, after I met nutrition expert Joel Fuhrman and signed up with Weight Watchers.

It's hard to believe that a moderately aware, reasonably well-informed person can spend half a century on this earth and still remain profoundly naive about something as basic as healthy eating. Yet somehow I managed.

Food—unless it happens to be sitting on my plate—isn't a favorite topic of conversation with me. Nor does the subject top my reading list. Until recently, the foundation of my knowledge was the Four Basic Food Groups from third grade. You remember those, don't you, and the chart with plenty of red meat, whole milk, white bread, cheese, and pasta? The only thing missing, as far as I could tell, was a piece of fried chicken and a Coke.

And so I wandered through life, eating whatever tasted best, whenever I felt like it, and congratulating myself for not topping off my latest pig-fest with a bowl of ice cream and a cigarette, like some folks. (Actually, I usually *did* have the bowl of ice cream.)

An awakening of sorts actually began a few years earlier when I attended a social event where I met some health food advocates and found myself lost in conversations about chemical pesticides, the use of antibiotics to fatten livestock, conditions at factory farms, and the nutritional excellence of kale and blueberries. Since I had little to contribute to these topics, I kept my ears open and tried to learn something. My eyes took in something else, however. These folks discussing what constituted the healthiest lifestyle had one thing in common: They were rail thin.

That made them pretty exceptional. Walk through any shopping mall or airport in America today and you'll see something very different. Surveys show that roughly 70 percent of adult Americans are somewhere between overweight and morbidly obese.

Yet these folks didn't talk about weight loss. Their passion was the superb health, vitality, and disease resistance that naturally accrues from nutritional excellence and an active lifestyle. Achieving and maintaining their ideal weight was merely a *by-product* of their interest in optimal health.

Hmm. I felt like I was onto something here.

Our generation is among the first people in history to have the luxury of bombarding ourselves with low-cost, nutrient-deficient, high-calorie food. Mix in a sedentary lifestyle, and the result is not only a reduced quality of life but a budding health-care crisis. According to the National Institutes of Health, obesity is associated with a twofold increase in mortality and costs society more than $100 billion annually. (Mayor Michael Bloomberg says more people in New York City now die each year as a result of obesity than as a result of smoking.)

The best medicine, of course, is preventative. Unfortunately, too many doctors are inclined to prescribe a pill rather than a healthier diet. Eisenhower warned about the military-industrial complex, but how about the new medical-pharmaceutical complex?

A stumbling block for many is that eating, the most basic of creaturely activities, seems to have gotten complicated in recent years. You can't listen to a food expert without hearing about antioxidants, saturated fats, polyphenols, gluten, probiotics, or omega-3 fatty acids.

And we're only just grazing the surface. Author and "foodie intellectual" Michael Pollan points out that nutrition science, which started less than 200 years ago, is today approximately where surgery was in the year 1650. We haven't even discovered all the phytochemicals and other micronutrients in our foods, much less how they aid and protect the body. However, we do know two important things today:

1. Populations that eat a so-called Western diet—lots of processed foods and meat, lots of added fat and sugar, and lots of refined grains—suffer terribly from obesity, type 2 diabetes, cardiovascular disease, and cancer.
2. Populations that follow traditional diets of high-nutrient, low-calorie foods suffer far less from these maladies. In fact, they enjoy a host of benefits including lower cholesterol and triglycerides, reduced stress, enhanced cellular repair mechanisms, better resistance to cancer, nonappearance of atherosclerosis and diabetes, a delay in the onset of several late-life diseases, and greater longevity.

That's a heckuva trade-off. Fortunately, people who get off the Western diet see dramatic improvements in their health—and relatively quickly. And despite all the conflicting claims out there, it doesn't have to be a complicated process. Pollan points out that a healthy eating regimen can be boiled down to just seven words:

Eat food. Not too much. Mostly plants.

Here's what he means . . .

■ *Eat food.* This sounds puzzling until you realize that most of us today eat not whole foods (fruits, vegetables, nuts, whole grains, and lean meat) but what Pollan calls "edible foodlike substances."

There isn't much profit in selling mushrooms, raw almonds, and collard greens. So food companies create—and grocery stores promote—higher-margin food products designed to appeal to our inborn preferences for sweetness, fat, and salt. However, it usually isn't healthy to eat things your ancestors wouldn't have recognized as food. That rules out Lunchables, chicken nuggets, Twinkies, Doritos, Go-GURT, spray cheese, Cap'n Crunch, and Krispy Kreme donuts.

The key is to consume naturally nutritious whole foods instead of processed foods with dubious health claims ("Half the Calories of Regular Potato Chips!" "Zero Trans-Fats!"). As Pollan puts it, "If it came from a plant, eat it; if it was made in a plant, don't."

■ *Not too much.* The scientific case for eating less than you currently do—even if you're not overweight—is compelling. Caloric restriction slows aging in animals, and many researchers believe it offers the single strongest link between diet and cancer prevention. The one exception to this rule is vegetables. The more you eat, the more you will lose. Dr. Fuhrman recommends eating a pound of raw vegetables and a pound of cooked vegetables *every day*.

■ *Mostly plants.* Vegetarians are notably healthier than carnivores. They also tend to live longer. You don't have to *be* a vegetarian—I'm certainly not—to recognize the benefits of *moving in that direction*. In countries where people eat a pound or more of vegetables and fruits a day, the rate of cancer is half what it is in the United States. And there is evidence that the more meat there is in your diet, red meat in particular, the greater your risk of heart disease and colon cancer.

In addition, *how* you eat is almost as important as *what* you eat. Pollan notes that the French consume all sorts of supposedly lethal fatty foods and wash them down with red wine, but are healthier, thinner, and longer lived than we are. Perhaps that's because they seldom snack, eat small portions from small plates, don't go back for seconds, and eat most of their food at long, leisurely meals shared with family or friends. These customs may matter more than any magical food combination.

Of course, what really matters is your everyday practice—your default eating habits. In my quest to get healthier and reach my ideal weight, I lapsed occasionally. (Okay, a bunch.) But I discovered that's all right. The important thing is not what you eat at a particular dinner party or at a certain great restaurant but how you eat day in and day out. No one wants to spend every meal obsessing about food. A relaxed attitude is important.

If healthy eating is something you or someone you love has struggled with, it wouldn't hurt to consider a complete system like Weight Watchers. There are plenty of proven weight-loss programs, of course, but in 2011 *U.S. News & World Report* published its first-ever Best Diets rankings. A panel of 22 leading, independent science experts ranked 20 different diet programs based on seven key factors: short-term weight loss, long-term weight loss, ease of compliance, nutritional completeness, health risks, and ability to prevent or manage diabetes and heart disease. Weight Watchers—based on healthy eating, physical activity, behavior modification, and support—finished at the top of the heap.

Whatever approach you choose, understand that the stakes are large. Adopting and maintaining a healthy diet is the first and most important step on the path to wellness. It helps protect against heart disease, stroke, some forms of cancer, and even the mental decline commonly associated with old age. It can lower your blood pressure, prevent or reverse diabetes, and combat other weight-related illnesses, including depression. Better nutrition allows you to live a higher-quality, longer life, one full of laughter, activity, and enduring health.

Oh, and something else you may not have considered: you'll probably look better, too.

THREE WORDS THAT WILL SAVE YOUR LIFE

Talk about a model prisoner. . . .

In 1985, Fleet Maull began serving a 14-year sentence for drug trafficking. During his incarceration, he completed a PhD in psychology, authored a well-received book, became an ordained priest, founded a prison hospice program, and launched the Prison Dharma Network, a nonprofit organization that supports prisoner rehabilitation through contemplative spirituality.

Today, Maull works as a peace activist and personal effectiveness coach, lecturing at leading universities, in corporate boardrooms, in high-risk areas like Rwanda and the Middle East, and in what he calls "the forgotten world" inside our jails and prisons.

Maull has plenty of wisdom and experience to share. But he sums up his core message in a single phrase: Radical Responsibility. Maull believes we create both the good and bad things happening in our lives. And it is only when we accept complete responsibility that we take the giant step from childhood to adulthood. Self-responsibility is the key to personal effectiveness in every sphere of life. Yet many choose to embrace the psychology of helplessness and victimhood, preferring to explain all their struggles in terms of the actions of others.

Like you, perhaps, I meet many middle-aged men and women who are still grumbling and complaining about earlier unhappy experiences, who are still blaming their problems on other people or "the breaks." They are angry with their parents, fuming at an old boss, still simmering over their ex-spouse. They are trapped in the past and can't get free.

Yet the great enemy of success and happiness is *negative emotions*. Fear, self-pity, envy, jealousy, and anger hold us back, tie us down, and suck the joy out of life.

Studies show that there are four root causes of these emotions. Once you identify them, you can begin to banish them:

- *Justification.* You can be negative only as long as you convince yourself that you are *entitled* to be angry. Unhappy individuals will always be found explaining and elaborating on the profound unfairness of their situation.
- *Rationalization.* Rationalization is self-deception, an attempt to create a plausible explanation for a socially unacceptable act (as in "If I turn this in six weeks late, no one will care anyway").
- *Blaming.* There is no quality more closely associated with unhappiness than the habit of blaming others for our difficulties.
- *Poor self-esteem.* Low self-esteem is generally characterized by a hypersensitivity to the opinions of others. No one wants to lose the respect of others, but conscientious people don't need to fret about what other people think.

Management consultant Brian Tracy points out that there is a simple antidote to these factors that create negative emotions. You need only say three words: *I am responsible.* Whether your problem is joblessness, addiction, overspending, obesity, or a damaged personal relationship, you move closer to a solution the moment you take ownership.

It is impossible to say "I am responsible" and still feel angry. The very act of taking responsibility short-circuits and cancels out negative emotions. As Tracy says, "Every time you blame someone else or make excuses, you give your power away. You feel weakened and diminished. Without the acceptance of complete personal responsibility, no progress is possible. However, once you accept total responsibility for your life, there are no limits to what you can be, do, and have."

Yet many would rather train for the Boston Marathon in three feet of snow than say these words. Why? Psychologists say human beings have a natural propensity to accumulate pride and shun regret. Whether we recognize it or not, we tend to take responsibility for the positive developments in our lives and attribute unfavorable developments to others or circumstances.

This is not to say there aren't times when our lives are significantly influenced by outside forces. Maybe you are a great worker who lost her job due to a corporate downsizing or the poor economy. Maybe your parents really were lousy role models. But victims don't create change. It's only when you choose to focus on what you can do and how you should act that you gain power.

Businesses and other organizations today are looking for people who are willing and able to think, who are self-directing and self-managing, who respond to problems proactively rather than merely waiting for someone else's solutions.

A study done in New York a few years ago found that people who ranked in the top 3 percent in every field had a special attitude that set them apart from average performers in their industries. It was this: They chose to view themselves as self-employed throughout their careers, no matter who signed their paychecks. These are people who set goals, make plans, establish measures, and get results.

Radical responsibility changes everything. It means you own your thoughts, impulses, feelings, and actions. *You* are accountable for the consequences they bring and the impact they have on others. This is not a burden, incidentally. It's a privilege and an honor to take ownership of your actions. It creates freedom and control. It gives meaning to life.

Self-reliance is the great source of personal power. We create ourselves, shape our identity, and determine the course of our lives by what we are willing to take responsibility for.

So if you want to change your circumstances and your life, just say these three simple words: *I am responsible.*

ARE YOU AWAKE?

I just returned from an eye-opening, two-week expedition to Southeast Asia, traveling with 38 other intrepid souls through Laos, Cambodia, and Vietnam. We saw, experienced, and ate an awful lot. Along the way, we also connected with one of the world's great Eastern philosophies, one that still speaks to millions, regardless of their personal background or beliefs.

Until recently, not many Americans considered Indochina an appealing travel destination. But that is changing. Laos, in particular, is a diverse and unspoiled country filled with gorgeous landscapes, ancient gilded temples (or *wats*), and millions of smiling people.

Our first stop was Luang Prabang, one of the larger cities in Laos and a UNESCO World Heritage Site. It lies at the confluence of the Nam Khan and Mekong Rivers and is among the friendliest and most sophisticated cities in Southeast Asia. It is also one of the world's hottest travel destinations. In particular, backpackers, eco-tourists and young people, many from Europe and Asia, view the city as a sort of traveler's Shangri La. You'll find loads of them jabbering away in the bars and restaurants on main street.

On our second day in town, some members of our group accepted an invitation to witness the Tak Bat, a time-honored tradition where hundreds of local Buddhist monks from nearby monasteries fill the streets before dawn to receive alms from the local people. It's a ritual that has been a part of the area's religious heritage since Buddhism was introduced in Laos in the fourteenth century.

Yet, to put it bluntly, unwitting tourists are trampling on the tradition. The Tak Bat is supposed to be a solemn ceremony where, in appreciation for their devotion, townspeople offer the monks—in silence and respect—fresh fruit, home-cooked sticky rice, or some personal gift. But starting a few years ago, murmuring tourists began crowding and following the monks down the street, cameras flashing as if Angelina and Brad had just hit the red carpet.

Some locals have also discovered that there is good money in selling potential donations—packs of crackers and overripe fruit—to eager visitors at inflated prices. Indeed, the monks were so inundated with "offerings" that young boys had to run alongside them collecting the overflow from their wooden begging bowls.

There was a bit of chicanery, as well. One townswoman insisted that we had shortchanged her $10 for the modest bowl of fruit we purchased. (I shook my head and gave her the fish eye, but given her insistence and my inability to make a compelling counterargument in Laotian. I peeled off an extra ten.) The overcommercialized Tak Bat, however, was a single blemish on an otherwise engaging tour of many of the city's historic sites and colorful shrines and temples.

Buddhism, of course, is one of the world's oldest faiths, with roots dating back to India in the sixth century B.C.E. The life of the Buddha, which means literally "the Awakened One," is not known in any verifiable detail. But, according to tradition, he was an ordinary man named Siddhartha Gautama who attained enlightenment and taught others how they, too, could escape the suffering that is part of every human life.

He contended that happiness and peace of mind elude us because of our attachments and cravings: for status, luxury, reputation, material goods, and temporary satisfactions. He taught that these cravings could be overcome by following the Eightfold Path: Right Understanding, Right Thought, Right Speech, Right Action, Right Livelihood, Right Effort, Right Mindfulness, and Right Concentration.

In addition to being the predominant religion in Southeast Asia, Buddhism is growing rapidly in the West. Part of this is due to its decidedly ecumenical flavor. When the Dalai Lama visited my hometown of Charlottesville last year, he emphasized to listeners that it is unimportant whether you are a Buddhist. "What matters is that you show kindness and compassion."

This sentiment is at the core of every religion, of course. Still, it's hard to imagine many other religious leaders saying it isn't important what you believe, only how you behave.

Buddhism resonates with many in our increasingly secular culture. It makes no speculations about the nature of divinity or the origins of the universe. That's why some refer to it not as a religion or even a philosophy but rather "a science of the mind." The sayings of the Buddha tend to appeal to those of any religious faith—or none:

- Speak or act with an impure mind and trouble will follow you, as the cart follows the ox.
- Peace comes from within. Do not seek it without.
- I do not believe in a fate that falls on men however they act; but I do believe in a fate that falls on them unless they act.
- A dog is not considered a good dog because he is a good barker. A man is not considered a good man because he is a good talker.
- However many holy words you read, however many you speak, what good will they do you if you do not act upon them?
- Thousands of candles can be lit from a single candle, and the life of the candle will not be shortened. Happiness never decreases by being shared.
- Just as a solid rock is not shaken by the storm, even so the wise are not affected by praise or blame.
- Contentment is the greatest wealth.
- I never see what has been done; I only see what remains to be done.
- You will not be punished for your anger. You will be punished by your anger.
- Though one may conquer a thousand times a thousand men in battle, yet he is the noblest victor who conquers himself.

- The most essential prayer is patience.
- There are only two mistakes one can make along the road to Truth: not going all the way, and not starting.
- To understand everything is to forgive everything.
- Believe nothing, no matter where you read it, or who said it, no matter if I have said it, unless it agrees with your own reason and common sense.
- Your work is to discover your work and then with all your heart to give yourself to it.
- You too shall pass away. Knowing this, how can you quarrel?

Buddhist teachings have influenced millions, not just adherents in the East, but many of the greatest thinkers in the West, including Transcendentalists Ralph Waldo Emerson and Henry David Thoreau, psychologist William James, and that old crepehanger himself—German philosopher Arthur Schopenhauer.

The Buddha encouraged followers to develop their perspective though meditation and empathy. His goal? To wake us from our reverie and make us realize the impermanence of all things and the importance of easing the suffering of others. His integrity and clarity had a powerful impact on everyone he met. According to the Pali Canon, which dates back to 29 B.C.E.:

When the Buddha began to wander around India shortly after his enlightenment, he encountered several men who recognized him as an extraordinary being.

They asked him, "Are you a god?"
"No," he said.
"Are you a saint?"
"No."
"Are you a prophet?"
"No," he said again.
"Well," they asked, "what are you then?"
The Buddha smiled. "I am awake."

The One Factor That Changes Everything

A single factor overwhelmingly determines your success in life.

That factor maximizes your talent and intelligence. It minimizes roadblocks and negative circumstances. It determines your physical health and financial security. It colors your personal and professional relationships. It affects your well-being and longevity.

Without it, even people with exceptional genes, good luck, privileged backgrounds, or superior educations will falter. Yet those who have it experience less anxiety, greater happiness, and more life satisfaction. It even defines your character, determining the quality of person you become.

What is this all-important factor? Willpower, that special mix of determination, persistence, and self-control.

Studies show that willpower is a better predictor of academic success than IQ or SAT scores, a stronger determinant of leadership ability than charisma, and more important to marital bliss than empathy. If you want to improve your life, willpower is a good place to start.

Most of us recognize this. According to the American Psychological Association, Americans name lack of willpower as the number-one reason they fail to meet their goals.

200

The good news is that science is showing us how we can develop more willpower and improve virtually every aspect of our lives. Take my old friend John Reed, for example. John is one of the most focused people I know. He holds a medical degree and PhD and is the former chief executive of the Sanford–Burnham Institute in La Jolla, one of the nation's leading cancer research centers. He is the author of more than 800 scientific papers. (For years, *Science Watch* ranked him as the world's leading scientist.) And in 2013, John accepted the position of head of research—with a multibillion annual budget—at Swiss pharmaceutical giant Roche.

In addition to his academic and professional achievements, John is a committed triathlete, a loving husband and father, and one of the nicest guys you'd ever meet. How does he do it all? I asked him recently, and he ticked off six principles he lives by:

1. Set BHAGs (big, hairy, audacious goals).
2. Don't waste time—make every hour count.
3. Never stop learning. Be a sponge for knowledge.
4. Say "yes" far more than you say "no." Try new things/ new ways.
5. Exercise every day—no excuses.
6. Eat healthy all the time, consistently (no mammals).

Clearly, this works for John. (Heck, it should work for anyone.) Yet, aside from his natural abilities, what has really propelled John is indomitable drive and willpower. How can the rest of us get more of that?

Psychologists report that many of us live at the mercy of our cravings and desires, our lives dictated by impulses rather than conscious choices. We spend rather than save, sit rather than move, watch mindless TV shows instead of reading an improving book, and overeat instead of refraining, knowing that short-term temptations are undermining our long-range goals. Life becomes a struggle rather than an enjoyable challenge.

Yet we can change this, starting with a bit of self-awareness. Everyone struggles with some level of distraction, procrastination, or addiction. Even if you have great willpower in some parts of your life, it is probably lacking in others. I'm extraordinarily disciplined about saving and investing, for example, and pretty consistent on diet and exercise. But if you saw how I "organize" my office or the size of my ever-metastasizing music collection, you might run for the hills.

If we want to replace old habits with better ones, it is important to first recognize *why we lose control* and what we can do about it. In *The Willpower Instinct*, Dr. Kelly McGonigal, a health psychologist and lecturer at Stanford University, offers several suggestions:

- *Reframe your choices.* When you are tempted to act against your best interests, always stop and frame the decision as a conscious choice between immediate gratification and a longer-term reward.
- *Breathe slower.* Research shows that if you slow your breathing to four to six breaths per minute—10 to 15 seconds per breath—it shifts the brain and body from a state of stress to greater self-control. This makes it easier to resist cravings.
- *Take 10 minutes.* When you don't act on an immediate impulse, you give yourself time to pass on that first cigarette, second brownie, or third martini. Ten minutes is often all it takes to cause an unhealthy or unwanted impulse to pass. If your problem is procrastination, flip this solution around and tell yourself that you'll spend just 10 minutes tackling an unpleasant task, like cleaning the garage or filing your income taxes, and then quit. (Of course, once you get started you may not want to stop.)
- *Make it positive.* Shame and embarrassment actually undermine your willpower. So consider your challenges in a positive light. If you're trying to lose weight, for instance, think of all the tasty and healthy things you can eat rather than the long list of things you can't.

■ *Imagine your future self.* It helps to visualize yourself enjoying the fruits of your newfound self-control. You skipped the party and hit the books, so see yourself accepting that diploma. You stuck to your fitness regimen, so imagine sliding into your skinny jeans. Make a habit of asking yourself whether it's worth trading something you really value for a momentary pleasure.

■ *Exercise.* This is the wonder drug for self-control. Exercise calms you down, relieves stress, and acts as a powerful anti-depressant. Better still, exercise outdoors where you get the added benefit of fresh air and sunlight.

■ *Sleep more.* Sleep deprivation can make you susceptible to temptation, stress, and cravings. Even a single good night's sleep raises brain functioning to a higher level.

■ *Precommit.* Pay in advance for those music lessons. Splurge on an expensive gym membership or personal trainer. When you make it inconvenient to back out, you increase the likelihood of following through.

■ *Write down your goals.* There are few things that increase your personal effectiveness more than committing your goals to paper and reviewing them daily. This practice keeps your ambitions front and center and helps you avoid distractions.

■ *Meditate.* Neuroscientists have discovered that meditation leads to a wide range of self-control skills, including greater attention, better focus, and more impulse control. Research also reveals that meditators find it easier to lose weight or end an addiction.

■ *Be a morning person.* Self-control is greatest in the morning and gradually declines throughout the day (which is why you start visualizing that glass of merlot by 5 P.M.). If you have a willpower challenge, like mastering the piano or learning a foreign language, schedule it for the morning.

■ *Find a support group.* Studies show that good habits, positive attitudes, and determination are contagious. So, as much as possible, avoid associating with people who have the bad habits you are trying to ditch. Instead, seek out the company of others who share your goals.

■ *Be realistic.* Like me, you probably have friends who make annual resolutions to quit eating carbs, stop drinking, and exercise daily—all at the same time! No wonder they give up a week later. Any one of these is a serious hurdle. Big willpower goals like these are more effectively tackled one at a time.

Understand that we are all tempted by immediate gratification because our brains did not evolve to respond to future rewards. If your ancestors on the plains of Africa got a chance to indulge in sugar or salt or fat, for instance, they chowed down. After all, they didn't know when they might have the opportunity again. But in a world where sweet, salty, and fatty foods are plentiful and cheap, this biological imperative works against us.

Our rational selves and our tempted selves will always be at odds with each other. This is simply the human condition. But to the extent that we can control our desires, emotions, attention, and behavior, we can achieve the things we want and avoid the things we don't.

Willpower is simply the ability to do what you should do, when you should do it, whether you feel like it or not. (Successful people make a habit of doing the things unsuccessful people don't want to do.) Self-discipline is the key. It is the magic quality that makes everything possible, allowing you to rise as far and as fast as your talents and abilities will take you.

People like my friend John have made a habit of subordinating the self that seeks short-term gratification and instead developed that self devoted to a higher purpose.

Perhaps we all secretly crave someone who will make us do what we ought. That's all the more reason to strengthen your best supporter and greatest ally: the one in the mirror.

■ THE LIES WE TELL OURSELVES

I wrote earlier about Aristotle's idea of the "good life" and his conclusion that only virtuous living leads to lasting happiness. This is the moral of virtually every great novel or movie. The idea resides at the core of the world's great religious traditions. Parents everywhere try to inculcate it in their children.

We all imagine ourselves to be virtuous, of course, even if we seldom think of it in such explicit terms. But that's at least partly because we tend to be experts at excusing our own behavior when it falls short of the ideal.

In their tongue-in-cheek book *Rationalizations to Live By*, Henry Beard, Andy Borowitz, and John Boswell offer plenty of examples, ranging from the cringe-inducing to the hilarious:

I'm this way because of my parents.
Everybody does it.
I'll save even more money if I buy nine of these.
If we don't finish this second bottle, it will just go bad.
We're all going to die of something.
My wife doesn't understand me.
He's probably cheating on me, too.
I'm not running for "saint."
I do some of my best thinking on the golf course.
I'm only moving the ball to where it should have landed.

If I were in the hospital, I wouldn't want a bunch of people bothering me.
No one will ever know.
I've never been good with authority.
I only smoke at parties. I could quit tomorrow. This is my last one.
After a crummy day like this, I deserve these shoes.
After a great day like this, I should celebrate with these shoes.
With what I saved on this purse, I should buy these shoes.
All this shopping is good for the economy.
I'll do a better job on this if I start tomorrow.
You only live once.
He'll just spend it on liquor.
Skipping one day of exercise isn't going to kill me.
I'm just big-boned.
That's for the one you called "out" last game.
It's not sucking up to the boss if you really mean it.
I'm not trying to win a popularity contest.
I'm eating for two now.
What are the odds of a handicapped person needing this spot while I drop off a video?
It's deductible.
I'm only human.
They pay ushers to clean this stuff up.
My work was never intended for the masses.
I just don't test well.
Einstein had a messy office.
He'll thank me later.
It's not like he's never borrowed something from me and not returned it.
Ice cream is an excellent source of calcium.
This expense sheet makes up for my crappy bonus.
Finders keepers.
I'll be dead by then.
It's the thought that counts.
Nobody died.

And my personal favorite:

If God didn't want us to eat baby sheep, he wouldn't have given us mint jelly.

The authors point out that an excuse is a lie we tell others. A rationalization is a lie we tell ourselves. Of course, self-deception ranges beyond personal behavior to belief systems, too. Have you ever wondered how seemingly reasonable friends or relatives can hold such wacky political, economic, or religious views?

It's tempting to think they aren't very smart. But studies show just the opposite. As Michael Shermer, a historian of science and columnist for *Scientific American*, writes, "Smart people believe weird things because they are highly skilled at defending beliefs they arrived at for nonsmart reasons."

Psychologists call it the *self-justification bias*. We make decisions or arrive at certain beliefs for emotional reasons. We then go to work cherry-picking data that supports our view while systematically ignoring or filtering out contradictory evidence.

Nothing is easier, said Demosthenes, than self-deceit. Yet nothing is tougher to detect in ourselves than this penchant for self-justification.

How the First Americans Became Last

Every spring, when the air is full of birdsong and the smell of honeysuckle, I like to head off to my favorite getaway, a portion of the Appalachian Trail that runs through the Blue Ridge about 20 minutes from my home.

An afternoon tramp in the woods is a tonic. Without phones ringing, music blaring, dogs barking, or horns honking, the whole world slows down.

Living in town, you can forget about the fresh air, sparkling water, and green vegetation that make the Earth perfect for human habitation. Of course, there is a reason the outdoors seems so ideal. It was our first home.

Just ask a Native American. The land was fundamental not just to their ancestors' way of life but to their identity. They saw themselves not as above nature but as part of it, and appreciated its balance and harmony. They revered the woodlands, plains, and streams and celebrated them for the sustenance they provided.

European colonists took a different view. The North American continent was an empty wilderness waiting to be conquered. Their goal was to subjugate the land, own it, and develop it. There was an immediate clash of cultures.

According to archeologists, by the time European settlers arrived, the Indians had been here more than 10,000 years. During the last Ice Age, their ancestors had followed mammoths and other large game over a land bridge—now covered by the Bering Strait—from Asia to the Americas. Most hunted and fished. Some settled down to grow maize, beans, and squash.

But they were no match for technologically superior settlers with their guns, warhorses, ships, and steel swords. The Indians were soon displaced, either driven off their lands or defeated in war. They were plied with alcohol, swindled by bogus treaties, and pushed increasingly westward. However, the biggest killer was not the rifle or the sword but the lowly microbe.

Native Americans had never been exposed to Old World germs and so had no immunity or genetic resistance. Smallpox, measles, influenza, typhus, diphtheria, malaria, mumps, bubonic plague, tuberculosis, and yellow fever all took a devastating toll. Rubella harmed the fetuses of pregnant women and marked the children for life. Syphilis caused miscarriages and infected infants at birth.

Death wasn't always incidental. European settlers were among the first to engage in germ warfare. In 1763, for instance, the British military commander in Pennsylvania deliberately arranged for smallpox-infested blankets to be delivered to the Indians. Thousands died without ever meeting a white man or woman.

When the land was plentiful and colonists were few, some settlers sympathized with the plight of the Indians. In 1787, Congress passed the Northwest Ordinance, declaring, "[The Indians'] lands and property shall never be taken from them without their consent." But this magnanimity didn't wear well. The law impeded expansion and so became politically unpopular. By 1820, Congress passed the Indian Removal Act, forcing southeastern tribes to move to reservations west of the Mississippi.

More than 60,000 Cherokees died from disease, starvation, or exposure during the notorious Trail of Tears. Behind them came looters who plundered the homes and graves they left behind and stole their livestock. Any remaining Indians were stripped of property and left without recourse since no court would accept the testimony of a red man against a white one.

Indian culture was another casualty. Many Christian settlers viewed traditional ceremonies—sun dances, peace pipes, powwows, rites of passage, and "Great Spirit" theology—as pagan practices. Puritan and Jesuit missionaries moved in. Many Indians were suspicious of the black-robed, celibate men bearing gifts and promising eternal life. And their message didn't always take. In *Pilgrim at Tinker Creek*, Annie Dillard recounts an exchange between one native and a priest:

> **Native:** "If I did not know about God and sin, would I go to hell?"
>
> **Priest:** "No, not if you did not know."
>
> **Native:** "Then why did you tell me?"

The Indians were reluctant to surrender ancient customs, traditions, and religious observances. Far from being "mere savages," as land-hungry settlers and proselytizers imagined, America's indigenous peoples had developed sophisticated forms of art, elaborate political structures, agriculture, handicrafts, writing, and mathematics. They also followed, as every stable society does, a code of ethics handed down from each generation to the next.

Indeed, much of their collective wisdom can be found in Indian proverbs that echo views found in many of the world's religions and secular philosophies. In *The Soul Would Have No Rainbow if the Eyes Had No Tears*, Guy A. Zona anthologizes some of them:

- Always look at your moccasin tracks first before you speak of another's faults. (Sauk)
- It is less a problem to be poor than to be dishonest. (Anishinabe)
- Do not wrong or hate your neighbor, for it is not he that you wrong but yourself. (Pima)
- Strive to be a person who is never absent from an important act. (Osage)

- I seek strength, not to be greater than my brother, but to fight my greatest enemy—myself. (Pueblo)
- He who is present at a wrongdoing and does not lift a hand to prevent it is as guilty as the wrongdoers. (Omaha)
- Before eating, always take a little time to thank the food. (Arapaho)
- If you see no reason for giving thanks, the fault lies in yourself. (Minquass)
- Seek the ways of the eagle, not the wren. (Omaha)
- One has to face fear or forever run from it. (Crow)
- Wishing cannot bring autumn glory nor cause winter to cease. (Kiowa)
- See how the boy is with his sister and you can know how the man will be with your daughter. (Plains Sioux)
- When a man prays one day and steals six, the Great Spirit thunders and the Evil One laughs. (Oklahoma)
- If you dig a pit for me, you dig one for yourself. (Creole)
- Seek wisdom, not knowledge. Knowledge is the past; wisdom is the future. (Lumbee)
- Work hard, keep the ceremonies, live peaceably, and unite your hearts. (Hopi)
- Don't walk behind me; I may not lead. Don't walk in front of me; I may not follow. Walk beside me that we may be as one. (Ute)
- We will be forever known by the tracks we leave. (Dakota)

Virtues taught by the elders—wisdom, bravery, generosity, and honor—were designed to ensure intergenerational respect and the survival of the community.

But it wasn't enough. As clashes with Indian tribes turned increasingly violent, more white settlers began to agree with General Philip Sheridan's pronouncement that the only good Indian was a dead one. When Columbus arrived, it is estimated that 20 million natives lived on the continent. In less than 200 years, 95 percent of them were gone. It was one of history's greatest holocausts.

The Indians, like all people, had their own share of strife and rivalry. They warred with each other occasionally. And some staged brutal attacks on innocent settlers. But a people who once freely roamed the great expanse were largely gone, the rest confined to reservations. Today, their descendants struggle with extreme poverty, poor health care, high unemployment, alcoholism, and drug addiction.

Yet we can learn something from Native American traditions. Human beings need stories—grand, compelling narratives—to help orient our lives and find our place in the great scheme of things. The Indians found that in a spirit of interdependence and gratitude toward the Earth. They embodied a reverence for nature and an understanding that we are all connected, both to the Earth and to each other.

Their closeness to the natural world meant they appreciated the seasons and life's ephemerality. That's why the best Indian lore often sounds like poetry. In 1890, the last words of the Blackfoot warrior Crowfoot were, "What is life? It is the flash of a firefly in the night. It is the breath of a buffalo in the wintertime. It is the little shadow which runs across the grass and loses itself in the sunset."

THE TOP FIVE REGRETS OF THE DYING

Once we are no longer young, and therefore no longer immortal, most of us spend at least some time trying to figure out how best to live, so that when the time comes to die we can do so without regrets.

For this important task, we have two great human resources: the elderly and the dying. Yet we seldom avail ourselves of their insights. That's generally because we don't want to impose on the former or disturb the latter. (Or, worse, we are naive enough to believe they don't have anything to offer.) In my experience, most seniors are delighted to share what they know and are disappointed that they're so rarely asked. As one matronly woman insisted, "My epitaph will be *Once Again I Was Not Consulted.*"

As we grow older, we gain not just wrinkles and gray (or less) hair but knowledge and wisdom forged in the crucible of experience. You can't log several decades on this little blue ball without seeing a lot, hearing a lot, and picking up plenty of emotional scar tissue. Along the way, you develop not just perspective but understanding.

A life fully lived is one that has had its fair share of triumphs and failures, temptations, traumas, disappointments, false friends, and broken hearts, not to mention the pleasures and tribulations of parenthood. Once we reach *a certain age*, we have discovered— usually through trial and error—what works and what doesn't.

We have a better sense of what's valuable and enduring and what isn't. We may even have a few thoughts on how to grow old gracefully.

Many have found an ally in humor. Phyllis Diller claimed she was so wrinkled she could screw her hats on. Author and spiritual teacher Ram Dass decided he loved his wheelchair, calling it his *swan boat*. One impish resident of an assisted living facility noted, "If you are an old man and you go into a bar wearing pajamas, people will buy you drinks." And Mathilda Jones, a feisty 98-year-old spinster, told the *Houston Chronicle* in 1987 that she wanted no male pallbearers at her funeral. "If men could not invite me out when I was alive, they're not going to carry me out when I'm dead."

As we grow older, we gain a frame of reference unavailable to our younger selves. However, nothing puts a life in focus more quickly than landing on death's doorstep. Those who don't pass away suddenly are given a chance to do a final accounting, a true assessment that includes both satisfactions and regrets.

Bronnie Ware, an Australian nurse who worked several years in palliative care, routinely spent the last 3 to 12 weeks of her patients' lives with them. She listened to their stories and recorded their dying epiphanies in a blog called *Inspiration and Chai*, which she later compiled into a book. According to her, these were her patients' greatest regrets:

1. *I wish I'd had the courage to live a life true to myself, not the life others expected of me.* Wow, a biggie and, as it turns out, the single most common regret. Ware found that many folks get caught up in what well-meaning parents, children, spouses, mentors, or bosses want for them. Consequently, they found it impossible, as Joseph Campbell put it, to *follow their bliss*. Little is more important than finding your own path and accepting the responsibilities and obligations that come with it. However, it can take courage and determination to overcome the expectations of family, coworkers, or "society." The dying remind us that our time here is shorter than we think. Health grants us the freedom to

pursue our dreams. Once it's gone, we lose the ability to live the life that we've imagined.

2. *I wish I didn't work so hard.* I know what Ware is saying here but I wish she'd phrased it differently. Many people find meaning, purpose, and even a sense of identity in their work. It often leads to a feeling of *earned success*. Hard work can be one of life's great satisfactions, especially if it provides you with an opportunity to express your talents. So I would venture that working hard is not what the dying regret but rather working too much and losing balance in their lives. And workaholics often sacrifice so much for so little. A simpler, less materialistic lifestyle, for instance, enables shorter working hours, greater freedom, and more leisure.

3. *I wish I'd had the courage to express my feelings.* This isn't the case with everyone, of course. I've known folks who speak a river of confession. But others go through life with their opinions and emotions bottled up inside, often just to keep the peace. This is not only frustrating, it makes the individual feel like he or she is living a lie. Ware points out that, while you can't control the reactions of others, speaking honestly either raises a healthy relationship to a higher level or eliminates an unhealthy one. Either way, you win.

4. *I wish I had stayed in touch with my friends.* As we go through life, we never stop making new acquaintances. But, in my experience, old friends are irreplaceable. These are the men and women who have known us longer and better than anyone . . . yet choose to hang out with us anyway. Even golden friendships fade with inattention or neglect, however. And near the end of our lives, it may not be possible to find them.

5. *I wish I had let myself be happier.* It's sad how many people only realize at the end of their lives that happiness is an inside job, an attitude, not a particular set of circumstances. Worry and regret can poison a life and diminish the only time you have to be happy: right now. For it is always *the present moment.*

Why listen to the elderly or the dying? Because it is an excellent way of getting the wisdom of experience *in advance.* With each day, each passing hour, our future grows shorter. That's why it's essential to determine who and what are most important to us.

Ware's short list is a good place to start.

A Short Lesson
in Humility

I was driving along Route 250 when my son David, eight years old at the time, spotted Kohr Brothers, his favorite ice cream shop.

"Dad," he shouted, "let's stop for a cone!" It wasn't the worst idea I'd heard all day. We pulled in.

We got the usual—two vanilla cones—and grabbed our favorite spot, the bench just outside the front door. As we sat there, two attractive young women walked up and I said hello as they opened the door, but they were busy talking and didn't notice.

Ah, I thought to myself, 20 years ago they might have noticed, but not today. Back then one might have nudged the other, a brief signal, a silent recognition. But not anymore, I thought, a tad wistful. Too many summers had passed.

Just then, one of David's classmates and his father approached us from the parking lot. My son and his buddy quickly disappeared inside. I stood chatting with his dad for several minutes, shooting the breeze.

Within a few minutes, my ice cream was melting faster than the glaciers in Glacier Bay. By the time his friend's dad turned to go inside, the cone was disintegrating.

I took a couple of frantic bites but it was too late. The whole thing was coming apart in my hand. An opportunity lost, I tossed the sticky mess into the trashcan beside me.

As I wiped my hands, the two young women came back out of the shop with their cones and glanced in my direction. But they didn't just look once. They did a double take—both of them—turned and smiled broadly to each other, then continued into the parking lot.

My spirits lifted immediately. This was new. These women hadn't just looked my way. They had looked twice, then broken into big smiles. I reviewed the scene in my mind. Yes, they had definitely smiled. Maybe the old magic is still there, I thought. Maybe I've still got it.

Just then my son walked out of the shop, looked up, and shouted, "Dad!"

"What?" I said, taken aback by his tone.

He put his hands on his hips. "You have ice cream all over your nose."

AFTERWORD

An Embarrassment of Riches is the third anthology culled from more than 200 *Spiritual Wealth* essays I wrote over a five-year period for my investment readers at Agora Publishing. (The previous two were *The Secret of Shelter Island: Money and What Matters* and *Beyond Wealth: The Road Map to a Rich Life.*)

With the publication of each book, friends would often ask what they were about. It's a difficult question to answer about a collection of essays on a variety of subjects. I do believe, however, that there is an underlying theme: *the search for meaning in an increasingly secular world.*

Most men and women want to live not just pleasurable lives but ones filled with purpose and significance. Indeed, a lack of meaning often leads people to a kind of existential angst if not outright depression or despair.

For most of human history, people drew meaning and purpose from religion or cultural myths. (Anyone interested in the subject should explore the rich legacy of mythologist Joseph Campbell.) These stories told human beings how they came into the world and described how they should live their lives. But in the modern era, especially in the West, creation myths don't satisfy our hunger to know about our origins. Science does a much better job of revealing the natural history of the world and our place in it. But science doesn't provide us with purpose or meaning. Philosophy, religion, literature, and poetry do a far better job of that. The meaning of life, we find, is invented, not discovered.

Throughout these essays, I tried to share a few personal thoughts about what I believe matters and why. Each was originally written to stand alone and perhaps even spark a bit of inspiration. However, in reading them back-to-back in book form, I sometimes felt like I'd gotten an overdose of insulin . . . or a cup of tea with six lumps of sugar. No wonder writers tend to be cynical rather than optimistic. It's easier on the reader.

I said from the beginning that I hoped my kids would read these essays some day when they were older and reflect on a few things their father believed were worth knowing. I now realize this is probably a pipe dream. Not long ago, I asked my teenage daughter, Hannah, why she never responds to my e-mails.

"That's an easy one, Dad. I don't read them."

I guess that means perusing the old man's books is out of the question. However, I wrote these essays for me as much as anyone, really. I like the challenge of reading, researching, and abstracting. And this weekly deadline gave me an opportunity to distill some of the more interesting things I uncovered.

I once heard an interviewer ask historian David McCullough how he chose the topic for his next book. He replied that he knew only that he would pick a subject he didn't know much about. That surprised me at first. Most readers assume authors stick to subjects about which they already possess some special expertise. After all, "write what you know" is the first piece of advice given to aspiring writers and, as general prescriptions go, it's not a bad one.

But far more enjoyable, if you love to learn, is to explore a subject you wish you knew more about, then write about *that*. Essayists, in particular, tend to be generalists, not specialists. So I'm not afraid to admit that I'm no expert on insects or Confucianism or Transcendental Meditation or many of the other subjects in this book. However, each essay here is about something that interested me personally and that I wanted to investigate further. Writing them allowed me to do that.

Science fiction novelist Arthur C. Clarke once said that any sufficiently advanced technology is indistinguishable from magic. Today we live in a magical world, surrounded by miracles of medicine and technology. Our standards of living have never been higher. Life has never been safer, easier, or richer. To understand this we need only open (or raise) our eyes, look around and feel a heightened awareness, a greater sense of gratitude. Because you are heir to an embarrassment of riches. It surrounds you, just waiting to be discovered.

FURTHER READING

Alford, Henry. *How to Live: A Search for Wisdom from Old People (While They're Still on This Earth)*. New York: Twelve, 2010.

Armstrong, Karen. *In the Beginning: A New Interpretation of Genesis*. New York: Ballantine, 1996.

Atkins, P. W. *The Periodic Kingdom: A Journey into the Land of the Chemical Elements*. New York: Basic Books, 1995.

Baumeister, Roy F., and John Tierney. *Willpower: Rediscovering the Greatest Human Strength*. New York: Penguin, 2011.

Berman, Bob. *The Sun's Heartbeat: And Other Stories from the Star That Powers Our Planet*. New York: Little, Brown and Company, 2011.

Blyth, Catherine. *The Art of Conversation: A Guided Tour of a Neglected Pleasure*. New York: Gotham Books, 2009.

Bryson, Bill. *A Short History of Nearly Everything*. New York: Random House, 2003.

Bucholz, Todd G. *Rush: Why You Need and Love the Rat Race*. New York: Penguin, 2011.

Chernow, Ron. *Washington: A Life*. New York: Penguin, 2010.

Cohen, Richard. *Chasing the Sun: The Epic Story of the Star That Gives Us Life*. New York: Random House, 2010.

deGrasse Tyson, Neil, and Donald Goldsmith. *Origins: Fourteen Billion Years of Cosmic Evolution*. New York: W. W. Norton, 2005.

Elliott, Jock. *Inventing Christmas: How Our Holiday Came to Be*. New York: Harry N. Abrams, 2002.

Fadiman, Clifton, and John S. Major. *The New Lifetime Reading Plan: The Classical Guide to Western Literature*. New York: Collins Reference, 1999.

Flynn, Daniel J. *Blue Collar Intellectuals: When the Enlightened and Everyman Elevated America*. Wilmington, DE: ISI Books, 2011.

Fortey, Richard. *Life: A Natural History of the First Four Billion Years of Life on Earth*. London: HarperCollins, 1997.

Friedman, Milton, and Rose D. Friedman. *Free to Choose: A Personal Statement*. Orlando, FL: Harcourt, 1980.

Fuhrman, Joel. *Super Immunity: The Essential Nutrition Guide for Boosting Your Body's Defenses to Live Longer, Stronger, and Disease Free*. New York: HarperCollins, 2011.

Flood, Charles Bracelen. *Grant's Final Victory*. Boston: De Capo Press, 2012.

Fuhrman, Joel. *Eat to Live: The Amazing Nutrient-Rich Program for Fast and Sustained Weight Loss*. New York: Little, Brown and Company, 2003.

Gaustad, Edwin S. *Sworn on the Altar of God: A Religious Biography of Thomas Jefferson*. Grand Rapids, MI: Wm. B. Eerdmans, 1996.

Goodenough, Ursula. *The Sacred Depths of Nature*. New York: Oxford University Press, 2000.

Hitchens, Christopher. *Thomas Jefferson*. New York: HarperCollins, 2005.

Holt, Jim. *Why Does The World Exist?* New York: Liveright, 2012.

Hughes, Bettany. *The Hemlock Cup: Socrates, Athens and the Search for the Good Life*. New York: Vintage Books, 2012.

Isaacson, Walter. *Steve Jobs*. New York: Simon & Schuster, 2011.

Jefferson, Thomas. *The Jefferson Bible*. Washington, DC: Smithsonian Books, 2011.

Korda, Michael. *Ulysses S. Grant*. New York: Harper Perennial, 2009.

Krauss, Lawrence. *A Universe from Nothing: Why There Is Something Rather Than Nothing*. New York: Atria Books, 2013.

McGonigal, Kelly. *The Willpower Instinct: How Self-Control Works, Why It Matters and What You Can Do About It*. New York: Penguin, 2012.

Mapp, Alf J., Jr. *The Faiths of Our Fathers*. New York: Fall River Press, 2003.

Mosley, Michael, and Mimi Spencer. *The FastDiet: Lose Weight, Stay Healthy and Live Longer with the Simple Secret of Intermittent Fasting*. London: Atria Books, 2013.

O'Rourke, P. J. *On the Wealth of Nations*. New York: Atlantic Monthly Press, 2006.

Perry, John. *Lee: A Life of Virtue*. Nashville, TN: Thomas Nelson, 2010.

Pollan, Michael. *In Defense of Food: An Eater's Manifesto*. New York: Penguin Press, 2008.

Pollan, Michael. Food Rules: An Eater's Manual. New York: Penguin Books, 2009.

Rosenthal, Norman E. *Transcendence: Healing and Transforming through Transcendental Meditation*. New York: Penguin 2012.

Scruton, Roger. *Beauty: A Very Short Introduction*. New York: Oxford University Press, 2011.

Sheridan, Eugene. *Jefferson and Religion*. Princeton, NJ: Princeton University Press, 1998.

Simon, Seymour. *The Sun*. New York: HarperCollins, 1996.

Standiford, Les. *The Man Who Invented Christmas: How Charles Dickens's* A Christmas Carol *Rescued His Career and Revived Our Holiday Spirits*. New York: Crown, 2008.

Taleb, Nassim Nicholas. *The Bed of Procrustes: Philosophical and Practical Aphorisms*. New York: Random House, 2010.

Tracy, Brian. *No Excuses! The Power of Self-Discipline*. New York: Vanguard Press, 2010.

Zimmerman, Larry J. *The Sacred Wisdom of the American Indians*. New York: Watkins, 2011.

Zona, Guy A. *The Soul Would Have No Rainbow if the Eyes Had No Tears*. New York: Touchstone, 1994.

ABOUT THE AUTHOR

Alexander Green is the Chief Investment Strategist of the Oxford Club and author of three national best sellers: *The Gone Fishin' Portfolio: Get Wise, Get Wealthy & Get On with Your Life; The Secret of Shelter Island: Money and What Matters; and Beyond Wealth: The Road Map to a Rich Life.*

He lives in Charlottesville, Virginia, and Winter Springs, Florida, with his wife, Karen, and their children, Hannah and David.

Websites:
www.spiritualwealth.com
www.oxfordclub.com
E-mail: feedbacksw@gmail.com

INDEX